KNOWLEDGE AS CULTURE

Drawing upon Marxist, French structuralist, and American pragmatist traditions, this lively and accessible introduction to the sociology of knowledge
gives to its classic texts a fresh reading, arguing that various bodies of
knowledge operate within culture to create powerful cultural dispositions,
meanings, and categories. It looks at the cultural impact of the forms and
images of mass media, and examines the authority of science, medicine, and law
as bodies of contemporary knowledge and practice. Finally, it considers the
concept of "engendered knowledge" through a consideration of the complex
and often troubled relationship between women and science.

 The sociology of knowledge has sometimes been marginalized as a narrow
academic specialization. This lucid study reclaims it as an essential tool for all
serious students of culture in all its forms.

E. Doyle McCarthy is Professor of Sociology at Fordham University.

KNOWLEDGE AS CULTURE

The new sociology of knowledge

E. Doyle McCarthy

London and New York

First published 1996
by Routledge
11 New Fetter Lane, London EC4P 4EE

Simultaneously published in the USA and Canada
by Routledge
29 West 35th Street, New York, NY 10001

Routledge is an International Thomson Publishing company

Typeset in Garamond by Routledge
Printed and bound in Great Britain by Clays Ltd, St. Ives PLC

British Library Cataloguing in Publication Data
A catalogue record for this book is available from the British
Library

Library of Congress Cataloguing in Publication Data
McCarthy, E. Doyle.
Knowledge as culture: the new sociology of knowledge/E. Doyle
McCarthy.
Includes bibliographical references and index.
1. Knowledge, Sociology of.
I. Title.
BD175.M395
1995
306.4'2 – dc20
96–5489 CIP

ISBN 0–415–06496–1 (hbk)
ISBN 0–415–06497–X (pbk)

CONTENTS

ACKNOWLEDGEMENTS

Norman K. Denzin, Guy Oakes and Robert Perinbanayagam performed the valuable task of reading the entire manuscript and offered critical commentaries.

Chris Rojek, the book's first editor at Routledge (currently Professor of Sociology and Culture, Nottingham Trent University), consistently supported it and me from the proposal stage to its near-conclusion and offered me the unusual assistance of both a talented editor and a critical social theorist. Mari Shullaw of Routledge graciously and expeditiously assisted me in bringing the book to completion and into print.

For several years my work in the sociology of knowledge took me into other fields of study, such as the sociology of emotions and the symbolic interactionist tradition in American sociology. Special thanks are due to my colleagues of the Society for the Study of Symbolic Interaction and in the Sociology of Emotions Section of the American Sociological Association, many of whom have become my close friends. These organizations provided the social arenas within which my ideas were developed and tested.

To my friend and late colleague at Fordham University, Joseph P. Fitzpatrick, S.J., I must express warm gratitude for years of support and encouragement.

The principal arena—the "streets," so to speak—in which this work grew up was in the classrooms of Fordham University, where I conversed with students and was tested by them. In thanking them, I also wish to thank those teachers of mine, Kestas Silunas, Peter L. Berger, and Werner Stark, who extended to me an invitation to take up this tradition of inquiry; they are responsible for my interest and enthusiasm, not my weaknesses or conclusions.

INTRODUCTION
The sociology of knowledge and culture

The sociology of knowledge has occupied a preeminent (if sometimes marginal) place in the social sciences, for its core texts elucidate sociology's paramount claim that *society is constitutive of human being*. Whether in the writings of sociologists from the French, German, or American traditions, the sociology of knowledge argues that society's influence extends into the structures of human experience in the form of ideas, concepts, and systems of thought. Furthermore, since social life belongs to human conscious life and reflective capacities, one cannot significantly address human being without addressing what Arthur Child called "the intrinsic sociality of mind" (1940–1, p. 418).

This book presents the principal arguments of classical and contemporary sociologists as to what "mind's sociality" means, demonstrating that our discipline today considers this topic in very different terms than those of Marx, Durkheim, Mannheim, and Mead. Particularly during the decade of the 1980s, social science witnessed a revolution marked by its knowledge of and sensitivity to culture and language, a revolution signified best by the growing influence of works in linguistic theory, the structuralisms, and poststructuralisms. Works in the social study of culture and in "culture theory" have not only influenced the specializations of family studies, social psychology, criminology, emotion studies, comparative historical sociology, and social theory, but are also regarded by some as transforming the prevailing paradigms of social science. This is certainly true of the sociology of knowledge. Today, as I argue here, *knowledge* is best conceived and studied *as culture*, and the various types of social knowledges communicate and signal social meanings—such as meanings about power and pleasure, beauty and death, goodness and danger. As powerful cultural forms, knowledges also constitute meanings and create entirely new objects and social practices.

Nowadays, the sociology of knowledge is regarded by some as a subdiscipline that is dated by its particular emphasis on the "social determination of knowledge." Some consider it superseded by "culture theory." I do not. As I argue in Chapter 1, the thesis of social determination has to be brought into dialogue with a theory of the cultural constitution of human experience. Stated

1

in propositional form: human experience is constituted by both the content and the manner of its conceptualization, that is, by cultural knowledge in the form of a society's languages, its beliefs, its norms, and its world view. This proposition states, in admittedly abbreviated form, the central idea of the sociology of knowledge: that while the entire realm of mental products is socially "determined," everything that human beings experience is selected, arranged, and "priced" by the intellectual and moral judgments and linguistic practices of a social world. It is only through language, categories of thought, norms, and so forth that experiences take on a conscious and communicable shape.

Berger and Luckmann's 1966 treatise, *The Social Construction of Reality*, signaled a change in the field of the sociology of knowledge, redirecting it from the study of the social determination of ideas to knowledges, specifically the knowledges that guide the lives of people in everyday life. More important, their theoretical statement asked that the sociology of knowledge study those processes in which *reality is socially constituted*, thereby redirecting the traditional focus of the sociology of knowledge on social determination. What Berger and Luckmann actually proposed was that knowledge and reality (by which they always mean *social reality*) exist in a reciprocal or dialectical relationship of mutual constitution.

In this book, and in keeping with Berger and Luckmann's argument, "reality" and "knowledges" are discussed in process terms: *reality and knowledges are reciprocally related and socially generated*. This is no less true of the social worlds we inhabit than of the selves we possess: both exist as real for us; both our worlds and our selves are spun from knowledges that render them real and meaningful. Accordingly, *knowledge refers to any and every set of ideas accepted by one or another social group or society of people, ideas pertaining to what they accept as real*. Emile Durkheim (1909, p. 238) summed this idea up in these words: "the world exists only in so far as it is represented to us." Reality is as variable as the knowledge that people have about it. We have no "reality" at all, unless we have knowledge to tell us about it.

My own approach to the sociology of knowledge restores several elements that are conspicuously absent from the phenomenologically grounded theory of Berger and Luckmann. In particular, I have tried to recapture the political atmosphere in which knowledges are generated, such as portrayed in Karl Mannheim's work and in the neglected sociology of knowledge found in the work of C. Wright Mills—classic works that I find compatible with such contemporary writers as Michel Foucault and Edward Said. The work of this book, in part, is to reestablish at the forefront of the sociology of knowledge the problem of the functions of knowledge in public life and in politics. This central theme is woven, either explicitly or implicitly, throughout the succeeding chapters.

Mannheim's sociology of knowledge first appeared in German in 1929 and was translated into English in 1936 as *Ideology and Utopia*. After half a century,

Ideology and Utopia remains a classic work that still engages and excites readers in a manner not unlike *The Sociological Imagination* (1959) by the American sociologist Mills, whose work was vitally linked to Mannheim's own. Mannheim sought to uncover the active roots of thinking—how it "functions in public life and in politics as an instrument of collective action." He referred to this "pragmatic point of view" (1936, p. 73) as one which recognizes that knowledges are part of concrete human actions and follow upon a group's emerging interests, values, and ethos.

In the tradition of Mannheim and Mills, the sociology of knowledge serves a vital public need. It inquires into the consequences that knowledges have in politics and in people's public and private lives. Toward this goal, the sociology of knowledge seeks to uncover the collective bases from which groups and institutions exercise and compete for authority. Such an inquiry reveals that currents of thought are *strategic*; they originate in group existence and collective action. This is a process in which people, acting with and against each other in diverse social settings and groups, strive to change or maintain events in the world around them. It is within this collective process to change and to resist change that ideas are generated. According to this view, the processes of "reality construction," linked as they are to what people know and communicate to each other, are enacted in a public arena. It is in such a public arena that what people think and know emerges; thinking and knowing arise out of people's confrontations with their changing worlds. In this political atmosphere, groups and institutions enter as authorities and arbitrators in the elusive business of defining and grasping part of social reality.

As said above, this book brings these issues back to the forefront of the sociology of knowledge: how groups, classes, institutions, and even entire nations of the world compete in the generation and direction of public opinion; the active function knowledges serve in public life as they engender and direct public opinion and action. In Chapters 2 and 5, for example, sociology of knowledge is presented as a method for examining the changing and conflicting interpretations of contemporary events, the shifting realm of what we call social "realities" (the quotation marks pointing to the relative and elusive status of what in fact is *real* and for whom). Sociology of knowledge examines how objects of public attention arise, how social problems come to be defined and the functions particular knowledges play in this process. For example, the conflicts of nation-states and parties, between church and secular authorities, of rising classes and such interest groups as women and people of color, of medical and technical élites asserting social agendas for the unborn and the dying are all concerned with the question: *Whose knowledge should decide?*

That battles are waged today over this question may not be as new as we might think. What *is* decisively new today is not only the democratic ethos that tolerates and even invites such conflicts, but also the fact that the stage on which battles are waged is immediately visible to all (instantly so, and for

3

permanent record and instant replay). What people know and what they think are events played out in the public arena, often and before innumerable audiences. The "media event" only dramatizes Mannheim's contention that the question "What is reality?" is both urgent to our present condition and preeminently suited to sociological inquiry.

Whether directly concerned with the public and political roles of knowledge or with other topics, such as the importance of language and social relations, the point of view I adopt throughout this book is an action-oriented theory of mind. In this respect, sociology of knowledge is closely linked to the philosophical tradition of pragmatism identified with such figures as the philosophers James, Peirce, Dewey, and Mead. What these thinkers share with sociology of knowledge is a view of mental life as a facet of human action. The human mind is conceived as an activity; mental attitudes and knowledge are always linked with action. Forms of knowledge are not inherent in the human mind but represent one of the many ways of being and thinking, one of the ways human beings carve out a reality. In turn, ways of thinking emerge from our interest in a reality. Knowing is interested activity. No knowledge of reality is possible or even conceivable that is determined by things in themselves. Pragmatists borrowed from the idealists the metaphor of knowing as "carving": out of a world brimming with indeterminacy, human actors carve determinate objects, thus enabling action to proceed (Shalin 1986, p. 10). Knowledge and experience are coterminous—they arise and develop simultaneously in human acts. According to the American pragmatist George Herbert Mead, whose work is discussed in Chapter 4 along with a number of contemporary writers on human agency, the human mind is best grasped as a capacity for action and involves the distinctly human capability of experiencing within consciousness, in the form of language and symbol, the social acts we engage in with others.

This pragmatist view of the social and active roots of thinking can be found in the writings of people from sociological traditions that are, in other respects, remarkably different. There is a decisive pragmatism, for example, in Marx, Mannheim, sections of Durkheim, and even Scheler.[1] Their pragmatist understanding of knowledge rejects the idea that knowledge is a mirror of reality or, as Paul Rock phrased it, "an incision into an unchanging universe" (1979); nor is knowledge a kind of bridge joining a world of people and things to what people think about them, as if knowledge and reality could be regarded as separate and fixed poles.

The pragmatist theory of knowledge offers a number of challenges to the entire philosophical enterprise and its history. It also raises troubling questions about what Alfred Schutz (1971) called the world as it appears in the structures of everyday thinking, whereby knowledge is seen as a bundle of accurate perceptions. This is because both everyday actors and most philosophers are committed to the idea that knowledge has a real foundation, one that is unquestionably there, or one that is there for the deciphering.

Neither philosophers nor their mundane compatriots concern us here, except as striking contrasts with those who profess sociology's (and pragmatism's) understanding of knowledge, which holds that there are a number of vital functions that knowledges serve that have nothing whatsoever to do with clear thinking or with truth-seeking; those functions are precisely what interest the sociologist. Perhaps this sounds a bit perverse. I would agree that it is, since perversity involves turning aside from what is normally accepted as either right or good. Sociology of knowledge has long insisted that all forms of knowledge, no matter how lofty or authoritative, have human origins and feed and fatten off groups' interests and needs.

Knowledge's *other functions*, the sociologist's preoccupation, are not to be construed as secondary ones (nor primary ones, for that matter). Rather, sociology's claim is that these functions should be regarded with at least the same amount of attention and seriousness that are afforded other views of knowledge and mental life, such as those provided by philosophers, psychotherapists, religious gurus, and other virtuosi of the human mind and soul. These include the functions of knowledge to integrate a social order, to provide a coherent and meaningful sense of reality (and unreality) for human beings, to render and to preserve a person's or group's identity, and to legitimate action and authority. Sociology also has a special interest in the function of knowledges, called *ideologies*, to distort, justify, or mystify group positions and interests. In each of these examples, knowledges do not so much describe social realities as build and configure them.

Each of the book's five chapters addresses the collective functions of knowledge from within the traditions of social science that followed the classic works of Marx, Durkheim, and Mead: Chapter 1 describes and interprets knowledge and sociology of knowledge by using the sociology of knowledge itself. It establishes the boundaries of our discussion and the terrains that must be crossed. Chapter 2 considers knowledges as ideologies that mask or mystify social systems, organizations, and classes. In Chapter 3, the function of collective ideas and symbols as powerful, even mesmerizing, forces of collective knowledge and sentiment are taken up. Chapter 4 examines the functions of knowledges as instruments of communication; it extends the sociology of knowledge to include the realm of the self-concept and the self's knowledge of the Other. These human capacities for conscious communication presuppose an ongoing social process, a capacity to organize and to use language, social attitudes, and perspectives with reference to the self and the Other. Social life provides the stuff (words, gestures, attitudes) out of which conscious life develops. It provides the special "languages of the self" that shape particular forms and experiences of the self.

A discussion of feminist views in Chapter 5 reveals knowledges as preeminent vehicles of domination, bearing the mark of a culture, a class, a race, a gender. Feminist writers have been principally concerned with the knowledges produced in the highly specialized realms of literature, philosophy, and the sciences. They challenge the idea that the theories and methods of these disciplines are free from the marks of ideology, of male hegemony. Feminism undermines the traditional idea of science as a privileged way of producing an objective, reliable, and value-free body of ideas. In this, feminism is compatible with sociology of knowledge and its view of knowledge as an adjunct of action and, as Mills (1939, p. 677) argued, a system of social control.

With each of the topics taken up, different though they may be, knowledges are consequential in generating what we know social reality to be; in providing us with a sense of social unity, spurious or not; in creating and sustaining forms of domination, legitimate or illegitimate; in rendering our personal lives and relations meaningful (or, at least, meaningful enough). The collective functions of knowledge have to do with the establishment of social reality through an ongoing and relatively precarious social process. To paraphrase John Dewey, *social reality exists in transmission*, in the knowledges that render it real for us (Dewey [1916] 1980, p. 5).

If the sociology of knowledge achieves anything at all, it makes the matter of our connection with reality a rather complex issue. The entire question of what it means to know something is far more of a problem than it ordinarily seems. Human beings don't just look and see. Things are not just there. How we see, what we see, and what we make of what we see are shaped by the elements of our mental maps. Ourselves, others, God, time, space, and all the objects that fill the social landscape exist in knowledges. But not only objects, reality is human beings and their thoughts, evaluations, judgments, and their feelings, too.

For all of these reasons, processes of thought reveal more about the collective practices of people than about individual thinkers. Since thinking is an activity that presupposes communication and social intercourse, only in a limited sense does an individual think. As Mannheim observed, "it is more correct to insist that an individual participates in thinking further what other men have thought before him" (1936, p. 3). Our predecessors and contemporaries provide the patterns of thought and action that we are obliged to assume if we are to advance the human conversation. Durkheim and the "structuralists," whose ideas are discussed in Chapter 3, considered that it is the collective origins of our ideas and categories of thought that render a coherence and impersonality to our thinking and our ideas: "impersonal reason is only another name given to collective thought," since when we reason we employ concepts that bear the mark of no particular mind but of a shared or impersonal source whose qualities are always general and permanent (1915, pp. 446, 433–5). Collective ideas have a quality of rationality, what Benedict Anderson calls a "halo of disinterestedness," a "logic of misrepresentation" (Thompson 1986, p. 45).[2]

The ideological functions of knowledge to distort or to misrepresent social reality (discussed in Chapter 2) bring the voice of Marx into conversation with a structuralist (Althusser) and a poststructuralist thinker (Foucault). Despite the fact that the Marxist theory of ideology has often been viewed as incompatible with the sociology of knowledge, I argue that it is more compatible than incompatible. What is common to each is the argument that all ideas and consciousness can be explained by collective forces and factors located in the forms of social life and practice, especially social groupings. This argument forms the centerpiece of two otherwise diverse sociological traditions, one originating with Auguste Comte through Emile Durkheim, the other with Karl Marx and, more recently, with "cultural Marxism." The concept of ideology also provides the sociology of knowledge with the rudiments of a theory of collective motives: ideological distortions and mystifications involve political processes—they have to do with claims to power, and with claims to be powerful (Ricoeur 1986, p. 161).

The considerable differences of opinion on the precise dynamics of ideological processes can be formulated as two questions: *Are ideologies limited to the self-serving ideas of particular classes*; or, *Is distortion and mystification an inherent feature of all known societies?* In Althusser's words (1969, p. 232), *Are ideologies "an organic part of every social totality?"* Do *"societies secrete ideology as the very element and atmosphere indispensable to their historical respiration and life?"*

In Chapter 2, I argue for an understanding of ideology as a special type of knowledge—one whose voice is authoritative, able to rule on the truth and falsehood of knowledges. Ideologies claim a position of privilege, a position that grants to its possessor a claim of universality. Ideologies are absolutizing voices, passing themselves off as natural, as the only way of viewing things. All knowledges contain within them the seeds of ideological thinking. But some knowledges, because of their totalizing features and their ability to naturalize social reality, and to reproduce institutions of power, achieve more perfectly the status of ideologies. Ideologies succeed as ideologies by repressing the constructive function of knowledge, by hiding the social histories and circumstances from which ideas and systems of knowledge derive their logics.

In this book, the sociology of knowledge is portrayed as inimical to all absolutist claims. There are no transcendent observers, the sociologist included. Sociology of knowledge offers a counterpoint to realism, and to the idea that knowledges are tools for grasping a reality that stands on its own. Its methods are *critical*, in the classical sense of this word: sociology engages one in a continuous criticism of what it studies, including its own forms of knowledge and criteria of judgment. In its skepticism it is undogmatic.

Does sociology always succeed in communicating this critical perspective? Of course not. Only *at its best* can sociology draw attention to the relative and artificial status of knowledge and to its own social function as an arbiter of the current social scene. At its best, sociology sees itself as a configuration of the same forces that shaped the modern world. Furthermore, sociology is not without its own political and institutional agendas, its own mystifying and absolutizing tendencies. But these are fated to exist in tension with sociology's reflexive character, its most vital feature. Vital, because it teaches us that people's knowledge of society, whatever its sources, is always provisional and unfinished. *As a reflexive discipline, sociology understands that its own project is part of the social reality it studies, that a social scientific understanding of society is an integral part of what society is.*

Paul Rock (1979, p. 83) has summarized this argument, describing social reality as "the accomplishment of processes of knowledge. It has no ontological independence outside those processes." From this point of view, the science of social life is seen as an activity that contributes to the process of world-construction, of generating new objects of knowledge (e.g., deviants, social roles), of tailoring other objects in accordance with its own point of view, its perspectives and pretensions. Social scientists knowingly and unknowingly intrude into this and that part of social reality. Our theories and findings have practical consequences, such as when sociological descriptions are converted by laypersons into rules of conduct. As Giddens (1984, p. 284) has remarked, "Sociological descriptions have the task of mediating the frames of meaning within which actors orient their conduct."

This book's overall design also includes a view of social science as part of culture and "cultural production" (Peterson 1976; 1994). The social location of ideas and systems of knowledge is studied in order that the student of sociology develop a "feel" for the strategic functions of knowledge, the differences particular knowledges make for what people do and how they live. What are the consequences of adopting the knowledge and authority of science, medicine, social science, or psychology for how we live our lives? How do the formidable social and political roles of law and medicine play themselves out in our personal lives as parents and children? A critical sociology provokes students to ask these questions, to examine the *value of knowledge* as a group strategy or as an instrument for controlling social reality.

As I've said above, a good portion of this book draws upon the classical works of sociology and sociology of knowledge by Marx, Durkheim, Weber, Mannheim, and Mead. For this reason, the success of my argument depends, in part, on its ability to give these works a fresh reading, one that renders them effectively relevant to today's world. This is because all readings and inquiries are socially circumscribed. Reading and thinking are no less social acts than anything else we do, since they presume conversants, a common idiom, and a social world to converse about. My own emphasis on the pragmatist view of the social and active roots of thinking derives, in part, from my sense of its success as a way of reading the classics for students today, a reading compatible with the newer studies in language, knowledge, and meaning. The pragmatist view of knowledge, as Rorty (1979; 1982) and others have shown, moves away from classical and modern ideas of knowledge as *representation* and mind as a mirror reflecting reality. In its place is the idea of knowledge as action, a political and social tool. It is entirely compatible with newer studies in discourse theory that argue that languages of all forms imply social positions and perspectives from which people speak. Institutions, in Foucault's words, "prompt people to speak . . . store and distribute the things that are said" (1980a, p. 11). In the

8

final analysis, no reexamination of the classics is possible except from one's special vantage point, a historical location setting the terms of the exercise. As writers today portray it, reading is both a historical and an interpretive act.

Sociology's work must be judged *in situ*: its concepts and its insights develop out of and are addressed to the social worlds of its practitioners. Sociologists are not in the business of offering timeless truths. We are neither poets nor metaphysicians. Our discipline is really designed for *situational diagnoses* that allow us better to understand what is going on in the world around us.[3] As sociology of knowledge best demonstrates, the very concepts and models we employ have their origins in real life; they emerged out of a confrontation with the dilemmas of social living and carry with them our conscious and unconscious strivings. At best, we try to understand our own social world by unraveling its special history. But it is always a history taken from our own particular vantage point. Contemporary sociology begins from and returns to our situation, the one for which it was fashioned in the first place.

Mannheim's *Ideology and Utopia* opens with similar reflections: sociology's propositions "are neither mechanistically external nor formal, nor do they represent purely quantitative correlations" (1936, p. 45). Our concepts and theories "were created for activistic purposes in real life." He even outlines the specific social situations that "impelled us to reflect about the social roots of our knowledge" and to confront "the alarming fact that the same world can appear differently to different observers" (1936, p. 6).

This fact no longer alarms us. For most of us, our own contemporary predicament (as Mannheim called it) is not the loss of a unified world view, nor is it even the problem of objectivity. Yet I think that the problem of the social roots of our knowledge continues to press us as it pressed the generations of Mannheim in Germany of the 1920s and Mills in postwar America, but for very different reasons. If I may speak along with my students, our own uneasiness grows out of our recognition of the elusiveness of social realities in the face of the multitudinous competing images and sources that give us "the story." Our sense of the variety of stories, opinions, images is as fine-tuned as our sense of the power of knowledge, word, and image to create and to control social reality. It might even be said that the problem of the social roots of knowledge and thought is even more urgent for us today than for earlier generations. Never before were people's experiences and knowledges so directly linked to mass techniques and technologies. Never before were ideas capable of being instantly communicated across nations, classes, continents. In a very real sense, the problem and the perception of the "social construction of reality" is our own problem.

The sociology of knowledge provides a living curriculum for sociology in today's world. Yet, as I have tried to argue throughout these pages, it includes a range of concepts and theories that demands rethinking and rereading. Its ideas, central to sociology's modern and contemporary history, are needed to grapple with many of the global issues and problems of the contemporary world: inquiries into the meaning of emerging political and cultural styles of thought and their class and institutional origins; the authority of science, medicine, and law as bodies of contemporary knowledge and practice; the cultural impact of the forms and images of mass media, nationally and globally; the changing face of political and religious fundamentalisms in the world today. Sociology of knowledge is eminently suited to explore these issues and problems, *our* issues and problems. For us today, knowledges have become powerful cultural forces. How to begin to comprehend them is what this book is about.

1

WHAT IS KNOWLEDGE?

> The nature of knowledge cannot survive unchanged within this context of general transformation.
>
> (Jean-François Lyotard)

PRELIMINARY CONSIDERATIONS

The sociology of knowledge is not a specialized area within sociology like the sociology of the family or the study of stratification. Its ideas address the broadest sociological questions about the extent and limits of social and group influences in people's lives and the social and cultural foundations of cognition and perception. Its special place within sociology is not unlike that of its sister field, cultural studies, which addresses general sociological questions within its own distinctive approach to the broad range of symbolic and signifying systems (Williams 1981, p. 14; cf. Stehr and Meja 1984, p. 7).

Like all sociological endeavors that have lasted several generations in this century, sociology of knowledge bears the marks of a *tradition* of inquiry (Shils 1981, pp. 137–40), a handing down of key texts and theories, seen especially in both the continuity and the changes in many of its themes over time: the "social determination" of ideas, the relationship of "real" and "ideal" factors, and the notion of *Weltanschauung*.

As in any tradition, the grip of the past must find reconciliation with the current and the new. In the case of intellectual traditions, classic texts and ideas are continually reread and reexamined in accordance with a new generation's insights (and prejudices), its sentiments, and its most urgent problems; if this is not done, these traditions will fall away, be discarded altogether, or seen as mere vestiges of times past. This is the problem of entire societies as much as of idea systems, since the continuity of social orders and of systems of thought is something continuously achieved.

Take the writing of this book. A big part of its work is the revisionist task of presenting classical works and arguments in the sociology of knowledge as of interest and relevance to us and our world today—in some cases, pointing out their replacement by entirely new viewpoints. Revisionism requires a good

11

deal of selective reconstruction and, at best, a conscious literary sense of narrative, a bringing together of classic texts within contemporary formulations, both of which are meant to enlighten us about the particular social landscapes surrounding us. The revising of any intellectual tradition entails the reworking of the persistent themes with which it is identified.

Two themes have come to be completely, though not exclusively, identified with the sociology of knowledge. One of these contains the marks of an older social philosophy and its preoccupation with the problem that occupied Scheler and Mannheim during the period between the two world wars: relativism and the conflict of ideologies. The other theme sums up sociology's newer postpositivist phase and its concern with the ways that social worlds attain their meanings. Each of these themes will be elaborated in this chapter as a way of presenting the core ideas of sociologists as to what knowledge is.

The ways that sociologists have studied and defined knowledge have changed during the course of sociology's history and within a number of different national and cultural settings. Of special interest to the sociologist of knowledge is how the elaboration of these themes has marked changes in sociology's own history, especially its attempt to respond to features of its own particular social landscape.

SOCIOLOGY OF KNOWLEDGE:
TWO DIVERGENT THEMES

The two recurring themes that can be said to summarize the intellectual tradition of the sociology of knowledge can be stated in propositional form. They represent two seemingly divergent ideas about knowledge's place within a social order. The first proposition, *knowledge is socially determined,* has dominated sociology of knowledge since its inception. Mannheim identified social determination as the principal theory of the sociology of knowledge (1936, p. 266; cf. p. 267, n. 1), and more recent statements by leaders in this field regard "social determination," or "existential determination," as the primary theme of the sociology of knowledge even today (Stehr and Meja 1984, p. 2; Remmling 1973). This is summarized in the famous formulation of Marx and Engels that thinking and consciousness are, from the very beginning, a social product ([1845–6] 1970, p. 51). That is, all human thought and consciousness develop out of real life, the actual social conditions that particular individuals share.

The second proposition, *knowledge constitutes a social order,* asserts that knowledges are not merely the outcome of a social order but are themselves key forces in the creation and communication of a social order (Williams, 1981, pp. 12–13). As will be discussed later in this chapter, the second proposition is currently the one that interests and dominates the concerns of many sociologists today. In fact, it is undoubtedly true that the perception of the sociology of knowledge as a field of inquiry that has seen better days is in large part due to

12

the conviction of many sociologists that the classical theory of social determination with which the field has been identified has been replaced by the prevailing idea of the "social construction of reality" through knowledges and the vast numbers and kinds of symbol systems.

The social determination of knowledge

The idea of the social determination of knowledge served as the first premise of such classical social thinkers as Marx and Durkheim and, in Marx's case, was intended as a philosophical and historical statement that marked a break from the entire tradition of thinkers in Germany's past and present. It is a statement regarding all facets of human consciousness and thought. Marx and the classical sociologists after him argued that, in the final analysis, knowledges (including a people's beliefs and systems of ideas) are profoundly influenced by the predominant forms of social organization. All of human thought and knowledge is determined by the productive activities of society, conceived as its highly visible and material structures of work, its institutions of labor and government, and its forms of technology (see Figure 1).

PROPOSITION 1: KNOWLEDGE IS SOCIALLY DETERMINED

SOCIAL STRUCTURE ⎯⎯⎯⎯→ KNOWLEDGE

● THIS PROPOSITION ASSERTS THAT ALL OF HUMAN KNOWLEDGE DEVELOPS OUT OF AND CHANGES WITH SOCIAL AND MATERIAL CONDITIONS.

Figure 1

In his writings, Marx repeatedly used the distinction between the material base or *substructure*—the realm of economic relations—and the *superstructure*—or the realm of culture and ideas (see Figure 2). It is stated in a famous passage from Marx's "Preface to *A Contribution to a Critique of Political Economy.*"

[T]he guiding principle of my studies can be summarized as follows. In the social production of their existence, men inevitably enter into definite relations....The totality of these relations of production constitutes the economic structure of society, the real foundation, on which arises a legal and political superstructure and to which correspond definite forms of social consciousness. The mode of production of material life conditions the general process of social, political and intellectual life.

([1859] 1975, p. 425)

KARL MARX'S DISTINCTION OF THE REALMS OF MATERIAL SUBSTRUCTURE AND CULTURAL SUPERSTRUCTURE

SUPERSTRUCTURE   including all of cultural and intellectual life: political, legal, religious, and artistic ideas and ideologies.

SUBSTRUCTURE   including economic relations or the "real foundation" of social life and history.

Figure 2

Despite the considerable differences between Karl Marx and the French sociologist Emile Durkheim, in the latter's writings we find a remarkably similar claim:

> [S]ocial life must be explained not by the conception of it formed by those who participate in it, but by the profound causes which escape their consciousness. We also think that these causes must be sought mainly in the way in which individuals associating together are formed in groups .... This postulate seems to us self-evident.
>
> (Durkheim [1897] 1982, p. 171)

These ideas have served as the guiding principles for sociological studies into a wide-ranging subject matter, all of it concerned with social influence and thought: the social factors contributing to different forms of religion, art, and law; the sociology of public opinion and mass communication; the sociology of intellectuals and élites; the social histories of world views; inquiries into the differing perspectives of generations; the social conditions giving rise to diverse thought styles and ideologies.

In one way or another, sociology of knowledge, and virtually all of social science for that matter, has been dominated by the emphasis given to "society" or "social structure" in understanding every facet of social life and culture. This emphasis guided the thinking of English-speaking sociologists until relatively recently. Institutions, groups, classes (what some sociologists call "social structure") and material conditions were viewed as primary forces in the development of the social existence and culture of a people. The realm of knowledge was studied as part of *culture*, which was understood to include language, art, law, and religion (cf. Remmling 1973, p. 16). According to this view, the entire range of social and material conditions comprised the first or primary realm, the real conditions from which culture is derived. "*Your very ideas*," we read in *The Communist Manifesto*, "*are but the outgrowth* of the conditions of your bourgeois production" (Marx [1888] 1967, p. 155, emphasis added). And further on (p. 158) we read:

14

Does it require deep intuition to comprehend that man's ideas, views, and conceptions, in one word, man's consciousness, changes with every change in the conditions of his material existence, in his social relations and in his social life? . . . What else does the history of ideas prove, than that intellectual production changes its character in proportion as material production is changed?

The idea of social determination also implied the *ontological primacy* of social existence ("*real* social conditions," as the phrase clearly asserts) over mentality, consciousness, and all of mental life. These real conditions were contrasted to the ideal ones, that is, things thought, imagined, and perceived. Everything thought or imagined or perceived was ultimately to be explained with reference to various facets of social existence. As Gunter Remmling described this dominant point of view: social existence was a reality "hypostatized as the ontological absolute," and (according to this realist logic) it excluded altogether the realm of mental phenomena, or it viewed them extrinsically "as phenomena . . . functionally related to" social reality (1973, p. 16). This primary social reality stood opposed to a realm in which things were ontologically less real, including the entire realm of representations: what people knew, thought, perceived, or understood. These representations were the various ways human beings perceived things and *not* the ways in which they acted or the ways they actually *were*. Until relatively recently, the idea that the entire realm of human conceptions serves as the *presupposition* of human action and human existence did not dominate the thinking of most social theorists.

The idea of social determination (and all that it implied) was so vital for the growth of sociological thought, especially in the English-speaking world, that it is difficult to conceive of a more pervasive idea in sociology's development. At its center was what is called "social organization"; everything else—modes of communication and interaction, culture, sentiment, knowledge, beliefs and ideologies—was a consequence of the forms of social organization. In effect, this operated as a major paradigm, was articulated in all the main branches of sociological inquiry, sorted out the "independent" from the "dependent" variables, and, despite protests from a number of leading writers throughout its history (C. H. Cooley, Robert Park, and Herbert Blumer were remarkably clear in their opposition to social determination), remained largely unquestioned.

The idea of continuous change has also been behind every statement and use of this first proposition, epitomized by Marx's statement that ideas and categories are no more eternal than "the relations they express. They are *historical and transitory products*" (Marx [1846–7] 1936, p. 93). Or, in the terms of his collaborator Friedrich Engels: the world is not a complex of ready-made *things* but never-ending *processes.* Things are "no less stable than their mind-images in our heads . . . the concepts go through an uninterrupted change of coming into being and passing away" ([1888] 1941, p. 44).

15

Sociological interest in knowledge has repeatedly focused on the changing and relative character of knowledges. Among other things, this special preoccupation with knowledges' changing character and social origins and functions was clearly different from philosophers' interests in the foundation of knowledge or of knowledge-as-truth. All knowledges, social scientists argued, were subject to change and were preeminently shaped by their social conditions. For sociologists then, the word "knowledge" has included all the possible types of knowledge identified in past and present societies: *everything that counts as knowledge*, whether religion, custom, tradition, magic, science, or psychoanalysis (Berger and Luckmann 1966). In keeping with this relativist perspective, a special concern of the sociology of knowledge has been how a people determines what is "knowledge" for them (the quotation marks signalling knowledge's variable status) and how they select what is worth knowing (Scheler [1924] 1980).

Robert Merton has written that "the term 'knowledge' has been so broadly conceived as to refer to every type of idea and every mode of thought ranging from folk belief to positive science" ([1957] 1970, p. 349). Since knowledge has been defined with reference to the social worlds people inhabit, knowledges are ideas that claim to accurately describe those particular worlds. In this broadest and simplest sense, *knowledge refers to any and every set of ideas accepted by a social group or society of people, ideas pertaining to what they accept as real for them* (cf. Berger and Luckmann 1966, p. 1). In the words of Florian Znaniecki ([1940] 1970, p. 309), for the sociologist at least, a system of knowledge is "what it is to the people who participate in its construction, reproduction, application, and development."

Given this broad and relative usage of "knowledge" by social scientists, the sociology of knowledge was intended to address a considerable range of knowledges, from pragmatic knowledges, including the various forms of information that are available to them, to the rarefied knowledges of, say, astrologers and psychoanalysts; from the mundane knowledges of everyday life to the knowledges of trained experts, such as systems analysts. However different the focus in each of these cases, sociology of knowledge has been principally concerned with how social groups and forms of social organization have contributed to the production and dissemination of these knowledges. Knowledges are subject to these two distinct processes: they are *socially produced* or generated, and they are *socially distributed*. The "social distribution of knowledge" refers to the fact that the knowledges that make up a society's "stock of knowledge" are possessed and used with varying degrees of clarity, refinement, and elaboration (Schutz 1971, p. 15, n. 29a) from individual to individual and from group to group. It is also the case that any given person uses many different kinds of knowledges as a matter of course, mixing information and common sense, drawing on both experts' ideas and on traditional notions, combining facts and observations with judgments and evaluations.

16

A special concern of the sociology of knowledge is how to account not only for the problem of how particular social worlds generate particular types of knowledges, but for how these knowledges enter the "stock of knowledge at hand" for the different groups, classes, communities, and types of social actors that comprise a social world. This means that knowledges can be studied as *extrinsic phenomena*: they are distinguishable from the particular human beings who think them; they are products of our collective lives, produced by specific groups, elaborated by institutions and professionals such as scientists, physicians, and theologians, reported and transmitted to us by a great number of different people, including parents, educators, politicians, journalists, and ministers. But knowledges are also possessed and used by any and all social actors as they go about the business of living. They are part of their very structures of thought and sentiment. In the idiom of our sister field, anthropology, the sociology of knowledge concerns itself with two aspects of a social process: first, *the social production of culture;* second, *the acquisition of culture*—how that culture, once produced, becomes the means by which people "communicate, perpetuate, and develop their knowledge about and attitudes toward life" (Geertz, 1973, p. 89).

The limits of social determination

More recently, since the mid-1960s, sociology has been distinguished by a growing interest in knowledge and culture as phenomena in their own right, rather than as outgrowths of forms of social organization. At the same time, social reality itself has been viewed not as an inexorable fact but as a problem, *the* fundamental problem of social science. Moreover, it is argued that social reality itself—meaning the entire realm of institutions, groups, and organizations—is best understood in relation to a society's culture or its symbolic or signifying systems—the various types of knowledges, symbols, and images that people use in the various domains of everyday life and that reproduce and sustain these very institutions. Perhaps it is best to characterize this contemporary phase of inquiry into the place of knowledge within society by stating that interest in the role of knowledge has developed along with the recognition that *social reality is not a phenomenon that exists in its own right but one that is produced and communicated*; its meanings are derived in and through these systems of knowledge.

As this formulation makes clear, this approach recognizes the difficulties attendant upon distinguishing "reality" from the signifying systems within which it is experienced and communicated. Social reality is formed out of the symbols and meanings that allow for its representation and communication by social actors. Reality is ineluctably symbolic because its very existence for human beings depends upon the means by which it is represented to us. This argument is a clear departure from what is commonly referred to as *realism*. In place of realism's view of knowledges as so many attempts to picture a reality

17

that stands on its own, is the view that knowledges offer us different and competing ways of grasping reality. Furthermore, knowledge and reality cannot be regarded as occupying separate or fixed poles, since knowledges and the realities they describe arise and develop simultaneously.

Although the critique of realism in social thought was prominent in the work of Simmel, Weber, and Scheler, for example, today it has come to dominate discussions in contemporary social science and social theory. One of its most recent influential formulations was Thomas Kuhn's *The Structure of Scientific Revolutions*, a treatise in the philosophy and history of science. Its concern was the idea of nature and the problem of the ways that nature was presented by various theories of nature. There are no such things as bare facts, Kuhn argued, even scientific ones, since facts emerge and are known by virtue of a form of thinking within which they can be received and accepted. In social science, Berger and Luckmann's treatise (1966) raised similar concerns by placing the problem of knowledge and reality within the broad range of signifying systems that form and communicate the entire realm of social realities. In the authors' highly influential formulation, *reality is something socially constructed*; that is, the sociology of knowledge should concern itself with the various ways people come to know both their social worlds and themselves as part of the province of reality. A significant feature of this theory was that "knowledge" and "reality" are aspects of what could be thought of as a single social process. According to Paul Rock (1979, p. 83), this theory was entirely consistent with the American pragmatist view that reality is "the accomplishment of processes of knowledge."

Cutting across a number of disciplines, another new and compatible challenge to realism developed. Summarized in the phrase *the politics of meaning*, it emphasized the pervasiveness of power and ideology with respect to both the forms of human consciousness as well as the realm of social practices. Its challenge to realism lay in its insistence that all speech and writing are sociopolitical acts insofar as these practices (speech and writing) reproduce the positions and viewpoints of speakers and represent a social dialogue between speakers and their audiences. These inquiries radically question the idea of the objective or free author or subject and the notion that any knowledge is so privileged that it can speak for everyone. These inquiries also describe the problem of the knowledge of reality as a problem of power, since all knowledges and the realities they purport to describe bear the marks of their distinctive social and political histories.

Similar recognitions as these have been expressed on less lofty fronts. For as Mannheim (1936) and Merton (1949) each reminded us, the problem of knowing reality is more commonplace than precious. It grows out of the mundane insights of an age. The sociology of knowledge is itself "the *systematization* of the doubt that is to be found in social life as a vague insecurity and uncertainty" (Mannheim 1936, p. 50). Today the problem of knowing reality impresses itself on the *conscience collective* in many forms: in the awareness of the fact that people's ideas and perspectives reveal their own particular station in life; in the recognition of the many, varied, and competing ideas and interpretations of a single event, along with a heightened sense of the power of knowledges to create and to control what is known; in the growing conviction that there are so many *versions* of reality corresponding to the near-endless numbers of special interest groups, each asserting its special right to express its own truth over those of others. Reality's many faces confuse and elude us. As Roland Barthes remarked in 1957, the difficulty of our times, "the measure of our present alienation," is "the fact that we cannot manage to achieve more than an unstable grasp of reality" ([1957] 1972, p. 159). We seem "powerless to render its wholeness."

Barthes.

Undoubtedly this perception of "constructed reality" has many social and cultural sources, among them our growing sense of the vital social function knowledges and information serve in shaping social and political relations on a national and global scale, and the fact that contemporary societies, like our own, consciously and strategically use knowledges to direct and to plan our social and political destinies. Knowledge, or, more accurately, knowledges (in the plural, to indicate the disappearance of a unified mental world), are both a personal and a social force and resource containing unprecedented social and political consequences. This is especially evident as we are confronted with the continual growth of new knowledges (scientific-technological, medical, legal) and with the developing technologies of knowledge, media and information technologies. With some hint of paradox we hear today of the elusive quality of social reality precisely at a time when technologies of knowledge are given over to the business of transmitting that reality with ever-greater precision.

1997: Japanese now endowed c right to transplant organs

These reflections are only meant to illustrate what might be called the worldly reference points that have stimulated the recent shift in sociology's imagination concerning the way knowledges are linked to what sociology understands reality to be. These reflections are especially appropriate in a treatise on the sociology of knowledge. For despite sociology's changes-of-mind concerning knowledge over the past 70-odd years, there is one insight with which it will probably remain identified, one repeatedly expressed by Mannheim (1936, p. 45), namely, that sociology's ideas are wrested from the raw materials of human living. They are formulated and refined in the "streets" of specific social worlds. Sociology's propositions, Mannheim wrote, "are neither mechanistically external nor formal, nor do they represent purely quantitative correlations but rather situational diagnoses in which we use . . . the same concrete concepts and thought-models which were created for activistic purposes in real life." The very questions raised (and not raised) by sociology about knowledge at different times and places are articulations whose reference points are the problems intelligible to all social actors (although neither seen nor interpreted the same way), as they strive to perceive and to interpret, with the benefit of their collective understandings, their particular worlds. Thus, as the social foundations of knowledge have changed in this half-century, as knowledges have become decisive forces themselves in our economic and technological development, sociology has begun to recognize the "autonomy" and "force" of knowledge *in its own right*. Similarly, as information and media systems have become part of our understanding of today's social control of knowledge and information, social science has articulated a theory that addresses the *transmission of reality* through its many and diverse signifying systems.

The social construction of reality

Berger and Luckmann's "social construction of reality" is emblematic of the second phase of inquiry into the place of knowledge within society, which we designate as the second proposition of the sociology of knowledge (see Figure 3). Since their treatise on the sociology of knowledge was published in 1966, the idea of a "constructed reality" has summarized a number of concerns of contemporary writers whose focus is best described as the problem of meaning and the use of philosophical, literary, and historical approaches to study the social construction of meaning.

PROPOSITION 2: THE SOCIAL CONSTRUCTION OF REALITY BY KNOWLEDGES

● THIS PROPOSITION ASSERTS THAT SOCIAL REALITY IS NOT A SOCIAL FACT IN ITS OWN RIGHT, BUT IS SOMETHING PRODUCED AND COMMUNICATED, ITS MEANING DERIVED IN AND THROUGH THESE SYSTEMS OF COMMUNICATION.

Figure 3

Interest in the problem of meaning is linked to a methodological framework that is neither causal nor explanatory (the attitudes expressed by the first proposition) but *semiotic*. The semiotic study of culture is directed toward the study of symbolic and signifying systems through which a social order is communicated and reproduced. These signifying systems and social practices are what make up a culture and its structures of meaning. This semiotic concept of culture, in Clifford Geertz's words, holds that the human being "is an animal suspended in webs of significance he himself has spun." Culture *is* those webs of significance, and the analysis of it is "not an experimental science in search of law but an interpretive one in search of meaning" (Geertz 1973, p. 5).

Today the pursuit of the *social origins of knowledge* that distinguished classical sociology and sociology of knowledge is being replaced with a decidedly new way of thinking about the problem of knowledge and reality, one that relegates the problem of origins to sociology's positivist past or to an older form of historical materialism. In its place is a concern with the social generation of meaning; its premise, that social and material existence are not distinguishable from a people's collective mental life. Material existence does not *precede* knowledge, language, thought, belief, and so forth, nor is knowledge "a secondary formation of experience" (Sahlins 1976, p. 147). According to this point of view, our mental lives are neither mere reflections ("secondary formations") of our society's structure and organization (the views of materialism and realism) nor the primary nor leading presupposition of our existences (idealism). The realities we live within and act toward are part of a social and productive process involving a socialized consciousness at every phase of its development. The types of knowledge we use, the images and ideas they evoke, the forms of classification are intrinsic conditions of all social action. According to this perspective, the distinction between substructure and superstructure, on which the sociology of knowledge was developed, disappears, since all of conscious life and thought is present whenever human beings engage in social activities of any kind, including activities known as "material production."

This, for example, forms the central argument of Marshall Sahlins's contemporary critique of the materialist conception of history (a conception here described as sociology's first proposition). This critique, like Berger and Luckmann's treatise, advanced the symbolic and cultural interpretation of social life and offered a new kind of resolution to the debates concerned with how material conditions and symbolic forms are related. His argument is that the structures of knowledge and conception are simultaneously products of action and action's presupposition. According to Sahlins's thinking, what and how we know are not the effects of material circumstance, such as "a particular technique of production, a degree of productivity or productive diversity, an insufficiency of protein or a scarcity of manure." Nor is knowledge conceived "as walking about on the thin air of symbols." (This denies the real effects that material forces have on knowledge.) The real point is that "the nature of the effects [of material forces on culture] cannot be read from the nature of the forces, for the material effects depend on their cultural encompassment ... the practical interest of men in production is symbolically constituted" (1976, pp. 206–7). What I understand Sahlins to be saying is that any human action is always and irrevocably symbolic *in the first place*. For human beings perceive themselves, their activities, and their worlds *as something*, and on the basis of these *conceptions* and understandings, productive activity proceeds according to a logic, and this logic is realized, tested, and confirmed in and through material actions. As to "material production," without symbols and ideas "material production" never amounts to anything at all. It never even gets off the ground. It never becomes filled with life, energy, interest, hope, and greed. It is precisely because "material production" is a collective idea and ideal (about "practical necessity," about a kind of salvation, about "making it," about progress and civilization itself) that productive activity takes on a life and a force of its own and grows up into "industrial capitalism," a society where economic factors come to be perceived as (and, indeed, *are*!) powerful, autonomous forces. "Historical materialism," Sahlins observes, "is truly a self-awareness of

21

bourgeois society—yet an awareness, it would seem, within the terms of that society"(p. 166; cf. Aronowitz 1990, p. xiv). On this, the early sociologist of knowledge Max Scheler would concur: looking backwards in time, he observed that "the *pre*-capitalistic world of Europe was certainly *not* determined by the primacy of economic factors, but by *another* law of history-generating processes existing between state and business, politics and economy, the power structure and the wealth of groups—and different from the way in which the capitalistic world has effected itself more and more forcefully in certain phases since its beginning" (Scheler [1924] 1980, pp. 56–7).

According to these thinkers, ranging from the age of classical sociology of knowledge to contemporary studies, the recent theoretical turn in social science probably corresponds to the contemporary phase of capitalism's history, a phase whereby the commodity form is as much a material production as it is a semiotic one—the Marlboro Man, the Honda Accord, Calvin Klein underwear, the Armani suit. In this era, "the production of signs dominates the production of goods." Such, at least, is the new shape of capitalism's productive forces, according to Aronowitz (1990, p. xxv). He and other social scientists have raised questions concerning the explanatory power of Marxism with its emphasis on the modes of material production in societies today—societies in which knowledge, technique, and the production of symbol and image dominate markets and productive processes and in which commodities serve as both signs and carriers of culture. These relatively recent cultural develop-ments have led both Marxists (such as Aronowitz) and non-Marxists (such as Daniel Bell) to propose that social science provide alternative models to those offered by classical sociology for understanding the preeminent place in today's world of cultural forms—signs, images, and knowledges. Some have described these new theories and models as sociology's "linguistic turn." Roland Robertson (1993) describes these changes as a general sociology-of-knowledge turn, marked by a focus on the ideational features of the social world or by a resurgence of interest in cultural forms more generally. The new sociology of knowledge can be seen as part of a larger movement in social science generally, distinguished by a turn away from materialist theories or theories of social structure, and a turn in the direction of semiotic theories focused on the ways a society's multifarious meanings are communicated and reproduced.

WHAT IS KNOWLEDGE TODAY?

Despite sociology's relatively new and innovative interest in cultural forms, the new sociology of knowledge[1] continues to view knowledges as highly relative social forms undergoing processes of continual change. "Knowledge" still pertains to everything that counts as knowledge, from folk beliefs, techniques and remedies for living, to religious ideas and collective opinions. Knowledges are also understood as expressing the collective experiences of entire societies as well as particular groups, classes, regions, and communities. Knowledges also

22

include, for example, the ideas, programs, and information developed and disseminated by a host of workers—professionals, such as doctors, scientists, and lawyers, or service workers, such as teachers, the police, and the clergy. According to Berger and Luckmann's influential formulation, "the sociology of knowledge must concern itself with whatever passes for 'knowledge' in a society, regardless of the ultimate validity or invalidity (by whatever criteria) of such 'knowledge'" (1966, p. 3). So, for this highly relative and diverse use of the term "knowledge," sociology is still indebted to its own tradition of inquiry. According to that tradition, knowledge means *knowledge-of-reality* or whatever information and ideas inform what we hold to be real and true about our worlds and ourselves. Knowledges are those organized and perpetuated ways of thinking and acting that enable us to direct ourselves to objects in our world (persons, things, and events) and to see them *as* something. In the often quoted words of W. E. Percy, when one knows something, one is "conscious of something being something" (Geertz 1973, p. 215).

At this point, let us define knowledges as *any and every set of ideas and acts accepted by one or another social group or society of people—ideas and acts pertaining to what they accept as real for them and for others.* This is the definition we first used in the book's Introduction. Its working premise is that social reality itself is in process and is formed out of the prevailing knowledges of a society or group of people. What makes a group of people a society or social world in the first place is what and how they think and what they know. In Mary Douglas's words, "Not just any busload or haphazard crowd of people deserves the name of society: there has to be some thinking and feeling alike among members" (1986, p. 9).

These continuities in the study of knowledge should not detract from the highly distinctive problems facing the sociologist of knowledge today, problems consistent with the idea that *knowledge itself is a historical construct*, forever changing its forms and the ways that it positions people within the worlds they inhabit. Knowledges cannot be divorced from the historically specific forms of social intercourse, communication, and organization. The highly specific and historical character of knowledge must also figure in our sociology as we think it and write it, reflecting the fact that today our consciousness is more global, more historical, and altogether more attuned to the powerful role of information, knowledge, and image in the making and remaking of social and personal realities.

In many respects, the new sociology of knowledge belies our collective sense of *difference* as the true mark of today's "social reality," a various and disparate reality, or what Asa Briggs has called our "disorderly 'intelligible universe'" (1989, p. 31). Difference manifests itself both in the range and the types of signifying systems, from written texts of popular press and journalism, to film, television, videos, and photographs, to the varied fields of discourse used, for example, within the institutions and regimes of business, police work, and medicine—what Stuart Hall has called the "heterogeneity of discourses"

(1980), the multivarious languages and practices through which we come to understand what is real for us and for others with whom we live and act.

Difference is also manifest in the forms and numbers of written and spoken texts that provide us with an ongoing sense of the everyday worlds we live in. Today's social realities are communicated to us in the forms of newspapers and popular press, the official reports of commissions (on crime, pornography, and public health), data provided by census bureaus, social scientists, political hacks, and so forth—texts produced and witnessed by the members of government organizations, administrative agencies, and such professional organizations as the American Medical Association. The growth and dissemination of these texts is both a mark of what knowledge is today and what *counts* as knowledge today.

Quite appropriately, today's sociology of knowledge is distinguished by a diversity of methods and subject matter, "knowledge" itself understood within the broader category of "culture," the entire range of symbolic and signifying systems; culture is studied in the many and diverse symbolic products of particular institutions and groups, such as those of religious practitioners, journalists, psychoanalysts, scientists, academics, and lawyers. Accordingly, culture includes the various types of knowledges, symbols, and images that people use in the various domains of everyday life. (See, for example, Swidler 1986.) This new sociology asks: What kinds of symbols and knowledges are used and by whom? How are they produced and disseminated? What do they teach? How are they linked to strategies of action and opportunity? Attention is given to the *production* of knowledge, in turn giving rise to studies of the observable properties of knowledges and symbols in texts, modes of communication, and forms of speech linked to specific institutional frameworks (Peterson 1976; 1994). In the words of Raymond Williams (1981, pp. 12–13), an early proponent of this position, "'cultural practice' and 'cultural production' ... are not simply derived from an otherwise constituted social order but are themselves major elements in its constitution ... it sees culture as the *signifying system* through which necessarily (though among other means) a social order is communicated, reproduced, experienced and explored."

According to this framework, the problem of *agency* (or, in social pragmatism, the self or social actor) is foremost in the articulation of what culture is and how it is produced and communicated (Swidler 1986, pp. 276–7). This is because contemporary understandings of culture seek to join the idea of structural determination with that of contingency: cultural production is a process involving social actors; therefore, it is neither inevitable nor entirely predictable in its outcomes. Culture itself, as James Carey (1988, p. 65) puts it, is "multiple, various, and varietal. It is this for each of us." The same can be said for the knowledge we have of social reality. It is disparate and dispersed. Today's knowledges come in variety packs. But they are also available to us in different sites and settings (hospitals, schoolrooms, meetings of local AA chapters, the offices in which we work), and they come to us via air waves and cables, billboards, and those glossy and scented magazines ads.

Today's studies of knowledge and culture are occupied, quite literally, all over the place, in whatever fields and sites of knowledge and cultural production there are—TV studios, scientific laboratories, therapeutic settings, police precincts and radio cars, boardrooms and classrooms—revealing a new conception of what systems of signification are and new ideas about how they are produced and what they do.

For the new sociology, the entire range of *culture* or *signifying systems* has been rendered problematic. Culture does not simply reflect the forms of social organization; nor is culture a mere expression of other social forms or material forces; nor is culture understood in holistic terms such as expressed by Durkheim's idea of the collective conscience. Culture is diverse, many-layered, and multicoded. Culture is not only discoverable in the "formal" institutions of law, art, and religion, but also shows its face in the "informal" sites of department stores, schoolyards, and fitness spas. Culture has entered the realm of the quotidian; it is accessible and observable for study in forms of talk, in family photos, in romance novels, just as it is enshrined in laws, doctrines, and literary texts. In keeping with today's more diverse and focused studies of culture and its production, culture is no longer understood as principally ideational—contained in ideas, symbols, or signs that reside solely or principally in texts (treatises of law and religion), or even in things (art, iconography), or in traditions. Rather, culture is studied as *cultural practices*, a term that refers simultaneously to collective forms of action and thought.

Stuart Hall (1980, pp. 26–38) has described the theoretical significance of this turn of the new social science: its problematic has become closely identified with the problem of the *autonomy* of cultural practices. The paradigm for studying the range of cultural practices, he claims, has come largely from structuralist theories (Althusser, Lévi-Strauss, Barthes): language is the theoretical and empirical model, one that is neither positivist nor reductionist (Hall 1980, p. 30); it is interpretive, not causal. As Paul Ricoeur (1986, p. 255) has noted in a similar context of discussion, social science's principal "attitude of analysis" is *conversational*. This attitude finds expression in today's firsthand studies directed toward the meaning of social life from the standpoint of its participants, and in the close studies of talk and gesture in small settings. These methodological attitudes also reveal an emphasis on the operations of both language and speech in the study of the social production of meanings. Language is the preeminent system and process for the study of how the process of representation occurs. Hall (1980, p. 30) explains the theoretical and practical significance of this linguistically based model for the emerging scientific study of culture this way:

Language, which is the medium for the production of meaning, is both an ordered or 'structured' system and a means of 'expression'. It could be rigorously and systematically studied – but not within the framework of a set of simple determinacies. Rather, it had to be analyzed as a structure of variant possibilities, the arrangement of elements in a signifying chain, as a practice not 'expressing' the world (that is, reflecting it in words) but articulating it, articulated upon it. Lévi-Strauss employed this model to decipher the languages (myths, culinary practices and so on) of so-called 'primitive' societies. Barthes offered a more informal 'semiotics', studying the systems of signs and representations in an array of languages, codes and everyday practices in contemporary societies. Both brought the term 'culture' down from its abstract heights to the level of the 'anthropological', the everyday.

This new view of culture is compatible with the contemporary apprehension that if "society" or "social reality" is anything at all, it is a multiple reality or, more commonly, a social world of enormous cultural diversity. This multiplicity or diversity is not without its problems and its politics. In fact, the idea of multiple and varied *cultural practices* expresses the point of view that in today's world, whether in the immediate sense or in the global sense, *reality*, *knowledge-of-reality*, and *meaning* refer to highly problematic phenomena. For as far as the status of reality or meaning is concerned, each of these are produced out of conflict and struggle. "To the extent that the symbolic is . . . the pragmatic," Sahlins writes, "the system is a synthesis in time of reproduction and variation . . . in action meanings are always at risk" (1985, p. ix).

The political feature of the social construction of meaning becomes apparent when culture no longer refers to *shared meanings* that reflect a people's way of life. Instead, *cultural practices* refer to the many institutions, classes, and groups that compete in the articulation of the social meaning of things, to the many sites and positions from which ideas and knowledges are developed, and to the conflicts arising out of the struggle to stage performances and to affect audiences. The contentious feature of cultural practices is also explained by the fact that what is said, claimed, or spoken is not, at any given moment, *ex equo*: some of it is "knowledge," other things are "facts" or "opinions," still others are "ideologies." The status of these designations is tenuous and, because of that, negotiable. For these reasons and others, the study of cultural practices makes evident the problem of the politics of meaning. It raises questions about how particular cultural meanings came to be produced, why, and by whom. It forces upon us the realization that the same cultural ideas, words, and images often mean different things to different groups. And furthermore, the meaning of something is continually subject to change both because social objects are multicoded and because there are a multiplicity of "languages." The cultural order becomes the outcome of historically diverse and conflicting groups. This is the shape of the new sociology. It offers a view of our knowledge-of-reality that, in comparison with that of our predecessors, is far more tentative, more open-ended, and more contentious.

2

TRUE AND FALSE KNOWLEDGES
The Marxist tradition[1]

Marxism, after drawing us to it as the moon draws the tides, after transforming all our ideas, after liquidating the categories of our bourgeois thought, abruptly left us stranded.

(Jean-Paul Sartre)

PRELIMINARY CONSIDERATIONS

According to one of the earliest and most commonly used theories of ideology, the Marxist theory, ideologies are distorted, mystified, and false conceptions that are opposed to knowledge and consciousness that are true, realistic, and objective. This theory understands power, status, and interests as the principal determinants of the consciousness of an economic class or a group whose thinking is ideological; that is, its thinking is politically and economically *interested*—its ideas rationalize the social and mental conventions that lend credence and support to its property and its power. According to this theory, ideological conceptions are to be contrasted with true or real conceptions of self, other, and world. At the basis of this idea is the accompanying one, that the clearest opposition exists between science and ideology, the scientist being free from the interested thinking of the politician, the partisan, or the bourgeois.

In today's world where the political and the ideological are, perhaps, more apparent to us than ever before, this classical theory of ideology is under fire, and some of its critics find the concept no longer useful for social critique and analysis (see, e.g., Lemert 1991; Seidman 1991). The reasons for these criticisms are many, and some of them deserve serious evaluation. However, these academically based criticisms of the concept of ideology fly in the face of the apparent ubiquity of ideologies. Whatever the merits of these debates, we ought to take notice of the phenomena the concept points to, especially when ideology is alive and kicking (or occasionally shooting) all around us.

Many of the critics of ideology theory point out, and I agree, that the theory of ideology is severely limited in its ability to account for the presence of both politics and cultural systems in the theories and practices of science and in virtually every social domain. The critics argue, for example, that "ideology" overrationalizes science while underplaying science's cultural and ideological features. More important, and more widely discussed, is the idea that power and interests operate in all domains and that reason itself is not free from the marks of class and group perspectives in its historical and social development. However, this pan-ideological position, one that views power and politics in virtually all features of social life and human transaction, is in danger of taking the critical edge out of ideology theory. It does this by diffusing its application to virtually all instances of group influence and claiming them as *political* influences, thereby surrendering its ability to distinguish different types of power and group strategies, as well as to distinguish those cases where power and politics are manifestly at work and others where they are not. There are many instances where the impact of a group or an institution may be profound but hardly political in the usual sense: so, for example, the effect of human rights monitoring organizations, such as Amnesty International, on public opinion. Popular culture offers other instances where modifications in collective behavior or *mentalités* have been brought about by an institution or organization without the uses of either political strategy or conspiracy (not that these activities are always absent from the way these organizations do business). Take, for instance, the formidable role of the Hollywood "dream factory" (especially in its heyday of the studios) in setting the imagery and ethos of twentieth-century America—not to mention the dissemination of "American culture" to the world by The Movies.

Reexaminations of ideology today undoubtedly arise in response to the recognition that the configurations of power and ideology are differently constituted in today's world from, say, the world of classical capitalism: today's classes, in the usual Marxist description of them as economic groups, have no monopoly on ideological forms, nor are all ideologies (in the sense of dominant or ruling ideas) to be limited to deceits or mystifications as in the usual sense of ideology; in today's world, systems of knowledge such as medicine and law need be neither false nor distorted, but the authority they effectively claim, the power they yield as institutions, and the élites they employ and protect certainly place them in the vicinity of ideological systems. (They are what the French Marxist Louis Althusser called "ideological apparatuses.") Nor does science operate at a remove from ideological systems. From our point in history we have glimpsed science's darkest moments (we may at least hope they are past) in Nazi medicine and in Hiroshima and Nagasaki, and we have come to understand that for us science can indeed work in the service of human horror and in the name of ideology. Scientific techniques can also be inextricably linked to "colder" and more bureaucratized forms of violence and of war, and to the state ideologies that accompany them. Indeed, ideology needn't be either fanatical or irrational; it can be practiced by the most cultivated and dispassionate professional, as much as by petty bureaucrats.

This chapter will recount some of the history of the theory of ideology from Marx to contemporary social science. Its argument moves in the direction of those thinkers for whom ideology is no longer a matter of a distortion of consciousness as much as it is a particular *use or practice*, where words and ideas are used in the service of power—its maintenance, assertion, or its defense.

That human beings continue to misrepresent to others and to themselves what they do and who they are provides a sound basis for the continued use of the concept of ideology for social and political analysis. Yet we would agree with some of today's critics that while Marx introduced and guided the inquiry into the social sources of ignorances, deceits, and mystifications, he left us unprepared to understand our contemporary ideological configurations, especially those of science in all its senses. Perhaps this is so because today's ideologies originate neither in a solid economic base nor in the region of class politics, but in a new environment of symbolic and hegemonic forms.

WHAT ARE IDEOLOGIES?

Ideologies are coterminous with modernity itself, with the disappearance of a unified world view, with the recognition that there are numerous points of view and these represent alternative political views and strategies. There is wide agreement (see, e.g., Hunt 1989, pp. 12–13; Billington 1980, pp. 206–10; Gouldner 1976, Ch. 2) that ideology developed as a unique concept in the midst of that febrile period of late eighteenth-century French revolutionary turmoil, alongside the modern idea of "the political." Both ideology and politics emerged simultaneously as ideas and as practices that took shape in accordance with new understandings about how people make their own history.

The word *ideology* connotes an enlightened secular standard of what knowledges should be—objective not subjective, rational not doctrinaire, and marked by equanimity not fanaticism. For this reason, and undoubtedly for less enlightened reasons, ideology has often been seen in clear opposition to science. According to these secular criteria, ideologies can refer to forms of knowing that prevail in other societies or historical epochs, which when seen from within our own and according to our own standards and ideals, appear to be out of joint or even inimical to our own ethos. According to the common uses of the term, ideology is often applied (rightly or wrongly, justifiably or not) to impassioned and doctrinaire group practices that are fueled by a good deal of interest and ambition. Fundamentalist faiths and racist creeds come to mind, but also anything that smacks of ethnocentrism or separatism. (Note the disparaging and condemnatory connotations of the terms "fundamentalist" and "racist," revealing a standard of belief and action that is supposed to be so clearly inimical to our Enlightenment heritage.) It is in these ways that ideologies appear to stand opposed to the standards of reason, restraint, and equanimity. (Whether or not these standards are patently pretentious, and can even function as ideologies themselves, is a matter that also will be addressed later in this chapter.)

Given the fact that modernity has been the progenitor of ideology, its uses and meanings difficult to extract from the frames provided by Enlightenment Reason, French revolutionary politics, or Marxism's ideology critique (to cite ideology's historical contexts), it is worth noting that ideologies appear to be everywhere on our national and global landscapes in the form of racial and ethnic conflicts, various fundamentalisms, reactionary politics, the growth of state violence and war, and neo-Nazi movements, to cite but a few. There are some very sound reasons for viewing these battles as ideological ones, in the sense that they represent the ideas and strategies of social and political groups whose interests and ideas are at odds with others, and who share a pressing political agenda. Furthermore, in the case of each of these groups, their ideas, programs, and actions are *believed in and lived*, not arrived at through some kind of rational critique, through consideration of evidence, and so forth. Ideologies are felt, embraced, and asserted. Ideologies take their life from conversions, convictions, from deeply felt realizations, from what appear to the ideologists as vital truths. It was in this sense that Hannah Arendt (1968, p. 167) referred to the capacity of ideologists to rewrite history according to their *ideas* of history and not its observation. ("An ideology is quite literally...the logic of an idea.") Ideologies "pretend to know the mysteries of the whole historical process." They are totalizing visions whereby a single idea orders all other thoughts and observations, assimilating everything into their own terms and perspectives and thereby claiming the right to pass final judgments over others from their own vision of things and from their own exclusive and well-cushioned seat of judgment. These descriptions bring us to another special mark of ideologies: *ideologies belong to the category of beliefs. But they are not just any kind of belief; they are contentious beliefs that become fully articulated and asserted in situations involving conflicts and interests, struggles over right and power.* In other words, ideas and beliefs *in themselves* are not ideological, but they can become so in practices of particular kinds.

We reserve the term "ideology" for those practices (including both acts and utterances) whose effects are directed toward a group's legitimacy and power. They mask a group's will to power and its accompanying strategies of action. Which is to say that ideologies tend to show their faces (either scrubbed clean or professionally painted) when the stakes are high in some objective sense; they involve struggles that are either central to an entire society or its principal players (e.g., its classes, its principal forms of capital or production). For that reason, a good deal more of the acts and utterances of U.S. pro-choice and pro-life activists are ideological than, say, groups of American farmers lobbying to gain advantages over labor groups in Congress. For one thing, abortion politics are rife with the politics and power-strategies of different and opposing socioeconomic classes and of America's two dominant political parties, and they are also fueled by other powerful players, such as the churches and other guardians of the moral order. Furthermore, the abortion wars enact a drama of justice and freedom, one that concerns the very meaning of life and motherhood. Such is the stuff that ideologies, in Arendt's sense of totalizing beliefs, are spun from. By contrast, U.S. farmers are better understood as "interest groups" whose concerns and politics are not only socially and politically legitimate, but whose efforts and interests are, in most instances, both more circumscribed and more clearly pragmatic. In the final analysis, ideologies, if they are effective as ideologies, must say something *meaningful* for those who practice them. They must matter in a vital way to those who espouse them and, at the same time, provide an action and a rationale for that action.

It is worth noting that while ideology is supposed to be at odds with many of the ideas and principles of modern societies, this has not stopped its advance within these societies, nor have our modernist judgments about ideology turned public opinion against ideologists and ideological movements. In fact, public knowledge about ideological practices has undoubtedly engendered a certain sophisticated use and exploitation of ideology in public life and politics. It is also the case that ideologies (at least contemporary brands of ideology) have advanced along with the secularist standards that, in many respects, oppose them and that secularist pluralism and rationalism even foster a tolerance for ideological expression. Certainly, the proliferation of ideologies, or what is called the *pluralistic* feature of our societies and its acceptance and tolerance of diverse peoples and cultures, has developed hand in hand with a polity whereby common or universal standards of truth and justice are supposed to mediate the conflicts arising over special interest groups and other groups whose own visions and politics are often inimical to the rights of others.

If ideologies are practices, they are *strategic practices*, concerned with power and the effects of both the positions and the claims of groups. One common strategy of the ideologist is to claim a special, a superior, place and function in relation to others' ideas and practices, such as the claim to be theoretical, rational, or spiritual and, on that basis, justified in acting as a final judge and arbiter over others. Understood this way, ideologists are by no means limited to members of political or religious programs or movements. For while ideologists certainly espouse ideas founded upon interests (who doesn't?), often enough they present themselves as supreme rationalists, or, in any event, they claim to exist above the fray of power and politics—a proclivity especially found among academics, intellectuals, and political leaders, particularly in those instances where they have a special claim to nonpartisanship. In this vein, Speaker of the House of Representatives Newt Gingrich once accused (and, I presume, without irony) his Democratic opponents in Congress of "wrapping themselves in bipartisanship," thereby adroitly disguising their own agenda and claiming to speak for everyone ("the good of the country," "The American People"—the shared vocabulary of the two-party system). In this way, ideologists disavow their ideologies, claiming to speak and act from purer motives, usually rational or universal ones. In fact, ideologies always involve an interplay of universal principles and special interests, the former used as a cover for the latter. Ideologists,

Kenneth Burke observed, have "pretensions to an ultimate vocabulary" (1989, p. 206).

The ideologists first described by both Marx and his imperial forerunner, Napoleon Bonaparte, and from whom the modern meaning of the word *ideology* can be traced, were those with special knowledge claims, a kind of pure knowledge. Ideologists were those system builders from whose vantage point all others could be assimilated and judged. In Napoleon's time the ideologues were the radical critics of the Empire—those dreamers, the advocates of Enlightened democratic principles, whose "diffuse metaphysics" would mislead the populace. Their ideology consisted in the fact that their ideas did not stand firmly on the foundation on which truth had to be based: reality itself, the real world of power and interests, a reality Napoleon believed to be based on a "knowledge of the human heart and of the lessons of history" (Williams 1983, pp. 154–5). *Ideologues* was a term of attack Napoleon leveled at this adversary— those regarded as unrealistic or "out of it" when compared to political men of action, whose particular access to reality was held up as a standard for all others. Napoleon was the first to use ideology in this pejorative sense, one that revealed a decidedly political criterion of what "reality" is; the practical experience of the politician became the standard for judging the adequacy or inadequacy of another's theories or ideas. Such a description brings to mind C. Wright Mills's "men of affairs," those sober citizens who parade themselves as hard-headed realists, epitomizing what Richard Harland (1987, p. 10) calls the Anglo-Saxon variety of common sense: "Anglo-Saxons have the feeling of having their feet very firmly planted when they plant them upon the seemingly solid ground of individual tastes and opinions, or upon the seemingly hard facts of material nature." Accordingly, ideologists do not base their ideas on experience but resort instead to ideas and deceits—to ideologies. As Raymond Williams (1983, p. 126) has shown, this conservative assertion upholds the "lessons of experience" over the ideologist's "rash" political innovation.

As Karl Mannheim (1936, pp. 71–3) first stated and Paul Ricoeur (1986, pp. 160–1) has more recently insisted, the history of the idea of ideology has never entirely lost its original political imprint, its denunciatory intention to undermine and to unmask a political opponent. Ideology is always (or almost always) a polemical term used about the *Other*. "His thought is red-neck, yours is doctrinal, and mine is deliciously supple"—as aptly put by Terry Eagleton (1991, p. 4)—which is to say that "ideology" calls into question the validity of an opponent's thought. Its usage is part of a political discourse, an instance of the political imagination, one whereby the very basis for the thinking of an adversary is brought into question. In the case of Napoleon, the opponent's thinking is deemed unrealistic, for it is removed from the experience of men of action. Its use in the political discourse of nineteenth-century conservative thinkers, critics of the Enlightenment, was so widespread that "ideologist" is still used today of supporters of liberal and socialist ideas or, as in Napoleon's usage, to refer to revolutionaries or fanatics. This meaning was eventually superseded by another highly popularized usage by Marx and Engels, the proponents of a theory of ideology that was equally derisive, a scathing indictment leveled against another set of dreamers, German metaphysicians.

Marx and Engels provided the first most systematic elaboration of ideology theory. Its continuity with Napoleon's *ideologues* lay in its intended use as a theory to attack and to unmask the distortions, illusions, and inversions that marked the philosophical idealism of the German Hegelian tradition. Marx and Engels's critique of these "German ideologists" was founded upon the standards of knowledge outlined by their own historical materialist method. Its centerpiece was the idea that ideology is the alienation of thought from life; ideologies are ideas that mask or mystify the real social being of the thinker. Ideologists are those "wolves in sheep's clothing," deceptively rational while actually seeking to accomplish some hidden agenda or particular political effect, such as the conservation of a balance of power or the assertion of a group's will in the face of resistance and opposition. The actions and motives of ideologists are often hidden from themselves, certainly not altogether, but enough to render themselves and their acts both utterly justified and reasonable to themselves and, they believe, to others. In many instances, ideologists are pragmatic, interested in action while appearing to be disinterested and even concerned for the common good. "Merely upholding the technicalities of the law," was the claim of then U.S. President George Bush and Attorney General Thornbergh, as they intervened in support of Wichitas's Operation Rescue in summer 1991. Using a similar strategy, pro-life advocates claim that they act on behalf of a "common humanity," which they share with the unborn. The point is not that all references to the law or to humanity are, *in themselves*, ideological. Rather, what's ideological is the claim (or, in some instances, the chosen strategy—either can operate) that a group belief is actually *not* that at all, but is a conviction that is embraced "for all" or "for the good of all." In Kenneth Burke's terms, the principles that are asserted here are "speciously 'universal,'" as, for example, when partisan convictions and politics are "wrapped" in Enlightenment's tricolor, signifying "common humanity," a rhetoric of universalism that announces its own version of humanity as everyone's. Instances of ideological practices such as these can be either unconscious and unintended on the one hand, or deliberately and strategically used on the other. In either case the effect is to idealize politically interested action. Idealizations like these, Burke (1989, p. 304) also points out, Jeremy Bentham called "eulogistic coverings" or "fig leaves of the mind," coverings that hide things from others and, most especially, from ourselves.

As these descriptions indicate, at the center of the idea of ideology is the idea of the intermingling of power and deception in the thinking of a class, or what could be called the problem of the *politics of representation*: how group interests, and especially a group's will to power, are inscribed in its thoughts, programs, and philosophies in a way that escapes consciousness. At the heart of the idea of ideology is a notion as important and fantastic as Freud's idea of repression and rationalization: what is most vital and important to us is forgotten or *repressed*, and what moves us to action is most often kept hidden from us. In the case of ideologies—ideas that mask group interests—these ideas not only serve to justify the practices of that group, but this occurs in such a way that it is kept out of consciousness. Ideologies both obscure and mystify the most potent facts about a group or a class, what it does and what it wants, especially how it imposes its will on its detractors and enemies.

Marx: ideology as unreality

Ideologies are a class's false conceptions or *false consciousness* of itself. The Marxist theory of ideology sets out to provide a materialist explanation for this false consciousness. According to this theory, all ideas, all forms of knowledge and consciousness, are in some way—and often in a distorted way—"interwoven with material activity." By "material activity" is meant the actual intercourse of people *as they exist* and as they are conditioned by the social and productive forces of the social worlds they inhabit.

Throughout the opening section of Marx and Engels's *The German Ideology*, the "real life" of "actual human beings," "as they *really* are" is contrasted with the conceptions (*Vorstellungen*), the imaginations and illusions that people hold. Ideology involves an understanding of how reality and *conceptions* of reality come to exist in opposition to each other—how consciousness fancies something other than what it really is. Using the idiom that Marx himself used, ideology is thought alienated from the real social being of the thinker, thought alienated from real life.

Ideologies are false or misleading *claims*, claims to be or to say something that is not true. For example, we can think of an ideology as a type of thinking that *flatters itself*, for it tells itself that it's better than it really is. As it does this, it doesn't know that it's doing this, since it's an unconscious process. It wouldn't be an ideology if it were aware of this flattery as it occurs. In an often-cited letter of Engels's written to Franz Mehrling (Engels [1893] 1968, p. 700), this unconscious feature of ideology is described: "Ideology is a process accomplished by the so-called thinker consciously, it is true, but with a false consciousness. The real motive forces impelling him remain unknown to him; otherwise it simply would not be an ideological process."

Ideological thinking flatters itself in a number of ways. For example, it presents itself to be purer than it is, to be grander than it really is, to be spontaneous or natural, to be thought up by a single individual, to be a statement of fact or of truth, when in fact it's none of these things. In each of these senses, ideologies are falsifications since they misconstrue or misrepresent thinking as something other than what it is. And what it really is, Marx argues, is consciousness of what *is*, consciousness of "existing practice."

The German Ideology is the first concise statement of historical materialism. For Marx and Engels, philosophy is the preeminent ideology, "claiming to have no history... of its own" (Althusser 1971, pp. 159–60). In this work, the authors' principal opponents, the "ideologists," are a number of German philosophers called the "Young Hegelians" whose failed attempts at materialist and socialist ideas are criticized as, in fact, highly abstract formulations of "consciousness," "self-consciousness," and "species-being." These abstractions are set in contrast with the *real* premises of historical materialism: "the existence of living human individuals" (Marx and Engels [1845–6] 1970, p. 45). The real bases of the ideas of these philosophers are the conditions of Germany and its history. Yet *as ideologists*, it had not occurred to them to examine how their German philosophy and their German reality were connected; nor had it occurred to them to examine the relation of their criticism to their material, economic, and political circumstances.

These German ideologists flattered themselves into thinking that their ideas were something other than consciousness of something real; they flattered themselves that their ideas "*really* represented something without representing something real" (Marx and Engels [1845–6] 1970, p. 52). If they had made such an inquiry, if they had glimpsed, as the young Marx did, their corner of the world as a place dominated by the problems of German idealism, they would have seen "the most mystified, the most alienated world that then existed in a Europe of ideologies." These are Althusser's words in his now-classic essay "On the Young Marx" (1969, pp. 75–6). In that work, Althusser draws together the abstract quality of the thinking of these philosophers with the alienated condition of Germany's history and its politics. "Germany's political and economic backwardness," he argues, was the world inscribed into the very structures of the thinking of the German philosophers: Germany's "historical inability either to realize *national unity or bourgeois revolution.*" "Germany's *historical underdevelopment* was an *ideological and theoretical 'over-development'* incomparable with anything offered by other European nations ... an *alienated ideological development*, without concrete relation to the real problems and the real objects which were *reflected in it.*"

Ideologies are *unreal* for they obscure, distort, or mystify reality. Ideologies belong to what Engels once called the "non-reality of thinking." But, as Marx and Engels were the first to argue, there is nothing haphazard in the thought of ideologists. For there is a logic and a *system* to this unreason, a *real reason* lying behind these unreal illusory notions and mystifications called "ideologies." These real motives that ideologies obscure are to be found in the foundation or *substructure*, the economic base, where class interests act as "the driving powers ... the real ultimate driving forces of history." The form that ideologies take "in the mind," Engels wrote, depends upon these material circumstances, "these driving causes of history" (Engels [1888] 1941, p. 624). This theory of ideology rests upon an understanding of the *realm of ideology* or superstructure, as explained in its connection with the infrastructure, the material productive forces of society. As stated in *The Communist Manifesto*, capital is this social force driven by the interests of its owners. Ideas and power are linked. "Ideologies are

35

false in the sense that they misrepresent, distort, or mystify what lies beneath them—a group's will to power, its own interests, its patently exploitative actions, or simply those instances or arrangements that put a class or a ruler at risk before the multitude. *Ideologies conceal motives and interests linked with power*; these, Marx claimed, were the real driving forces of history itself.

According to the Hungarian Marxist Georg Lukács ([1911] 1968, p. 66), the history of the ruling class of capitalism can be read as an *ideological history*, meaning a history of its persistent and desperate efforts to resist

> *every insight into the true nature of the society it had created and thus to a real*
> *understanding of its class situation* . . . the whole of bourgeois thought in the
> nineteenth century made the most strenuous efforts to mask the real
> foundations of bourgeois society; everything was tried: from the greatest
> falsifications of fact to the "sublime" theories about the "essence" of
> history and the state.

Regardless of where one stands on Lukács's reading of nineteenth-century bourgeois history, one can indeed understand that the history of Western modernity itself was a history made by the bourgeoisie, modern capitalism's "ruling class." The ideologies it fashioned—its philosophical systems, its sciences of economic and social life, its property rights and its individualism, its Romanticism, its psychologies, its subjectivist culture—can be understood as so many ingenious and powerful fabrications of itself and its own mission. For unlike the ruling strata of antiquity or the medieval orders of nobles and clergy that ruled under the aegis of a world view based on God and bloodlines reaching back to the reign of Charlemagne, the modern bourgeoisie had to invent itself, to fashion out of this entirely new industrial order what it was. Other classes and rulers in other ages acted invisibly, conscious of being neither social nor historical actors, cloaked by the formidable systems of religion and custom; the bourgeoisie had to *accomplish its invisibility* through ideologies, to mask the social forces whose existence and whose function were becoming more apparent with modernity's advance. This was the unique historical function of ideology within capitalism and the stupendous accomplishment of what Marx called its "ruling class." No wonder that Marx made the theory of ideology the focal point of his grand systematic reflection on the bourgeois order!

Yet the idea of ideology is not eternally valid. Ideology is conceived within the terms provided by the historical and philosophical systems that give it credence and value. Its application to human societies other than its own is an exercise fraught with difficulties. For example, critics of historical materialism from Sombart (1928) and Scheler ([1924] 1980, p. 56) to such contemporary writers as Sahlins (1976) have recognized that its application to premodern or to tribal societies is, at best, problematic, since the distinction of the material and the ideational is not a real distinction for those societies' inhabitants. In other words, the theory of ideology is closely implicated in particular historical conditions of the industrial capitalist order, and its validity is dependent on particular conditions of social and economic organization, such as the separation and autonomy of economic forces within the social order as a whole. In precapitalist societies, Lukács observed ([1911] 1968, p. 238), "economic life did not yet possess that independence, that cohesion and immanence, nor did it have the sense of setting its own goals and being its own master that we associate with capitalist society." The separation of the various institutional spheres and their increasing autonomy were also among the principal motifs of Weber's writings on the social economics of the modern order (Oakes 1988, p. 92). According to Weber's description of this development, different life-spheres came to be governed by different laws and principles, a peculiarly modern condition that fostered greater conflicts between the spheres as these achieved greater autonomy.

If ideology is conceived in the image of its time and place, as indeed it should be, the Marxist theory of ideology can be said to have reflected and systematized the idea of the autonomy of economic forces and, along with this, the idea that "all causality begins in the solid and practical" economic base (Harland 1987, p. 49). The *meaning* of ideas and belief systems, the Marxist theory claimed, could be read from the material domain. "Ideology" involved both the separation and opposition of ideas and reality, the "real foundation" out of which ideas grew. "Ideology" also furthered cultural ideas set in motion by industrial capitalism—what Ricoeur has called "a kind of realism of life," which we identify with this epoch, one where materiality is thought to precede ideas (1986, p. 5).

Ideology's expansion and diffusion

Behind Marx's theory of ideology lurked the notion that reality could be known and grasped directly, with neither distortion nor prejudice, or that false consciousness implied a true consciousness—a "knowledge without deception." Michel Foucault (1980b, p. 118), one of the mandarins of this post-Marxist era whose works are emblematic of a wide range of post-Marxist themes, has distanced himself from ideology theory ("ideology . . . is a notion that cannot be used without circumspection"). Behind the concept of ideology, he argues, we find a yearning for truth, a pure or a transparent form of knowledge free from distortions, lies, and illusions. For ideology stands in opposition to this "something else which is supposed to count as truth." Furthermore, the idea of ideology mirrors the notion that ideas are secondary to reality, that they are the effects of a material economic determinant. Such a schema banishes all of mental life from the infrastructure. The domain of real life is thought to precede the conceptions that we have of it, to exist *ab initio*.

One of the most important ways that Foucault's works allow for a new rendering of the modernist theme of ideology is through his examination of "truth" as an accomplishment of the systems of knowledge that rule a social order. "Discourses," knowledges with institutional moorings, in themselves are neither true nor false. For each society and each age have their forms of discourse within which truths are established. Foucault's analyses depart fundamentally from the Marxist idea of a hierarchy of determining factors, choosing instead to offer a "topographical" or genealogical point of view, studying: types of discourse, the technologies they spawn, the objects they render visible and invisible; and especially, "the techniques and procedures accorded value in the acquisition of truth; the status of those who are charged with saying what counts as true." "Truth," Foucault writes, "is a thing of this world." It is a political and social question. *The political question is not, as Marx argued, ideology. The political question is truth itself.* "Truth isn't outside power" (1980b, pp. 131–3), for we find it in the multiple and diverse ways that human beings govern themselves and others, and how they accomplish this governance "by the production of truth . . . not the production of true utterances but the establishment of domains in which the practice of true and false can be made at once ordered and pertinent" (1981, pp. 8–9). Accordingly, scientific knowledges such as biology, psychiatry, medicine, or penology can be analyzed as specific kinds of "truth games" related to techniques that human beings use to understand and to govern others and themselves (1988, pp. 17–18).

Such an analysis of how power and truth are linked takes the form of an analysis of discourse or *discursive practices* (Foucault's term), examining such things as archives and sites, new kinds of labor and public rituals where the genealogy of historical forms—"moral technologies" and "regimes of rationality"—come into being: the practice of clinical medicine; imprisonment as a general punitive practice; how mad people came to be regarded as mentally ill ("it wasn't as a matter of course . . . it wasn't self-evident"). Foucault's target is neither institutions nor ideologies, but *practices*:

> the hypothesis being that these types of practice are not just governed by institutions, prescribed by ideologies, guided by pragmatic circumstances—whatever role these elements may actually play—but possess up to a point their own specific regularities, logic, strategy, self-evidence and "reason". It is a question of analyzing a "regime of practices"— practices being understood here as places where what is said and what is done, rules imposed and reasons given, the planned and the taken for granted meet and interconnect.
>
> (1981, p. 5).

More than any other contemporary thinker, Louis Althusser probably changed previous ways of thinking about ideology, certainly for Marxists, but for non-Marxists, too. After Althusser, and in particular his 1970 essay " . . . Ideological State Apparatuses" (published 1971), an ideology exists in an "apparatus," the assemblage of institutional forms and practices that reproduce the conditions and relations of the industrial capitalist order: its schools, households, trade unions, communications media, its sports and leisure, its courts, its political parties, its universities, and so forth. Since ideologies always exist in and through these apparatuses, *their existence is material* (1971, p. 166). That is, while ideologies exist in different modes (actions, practical attitudes, speeches, gestures, texts, etc.), ideologies take up their "lives" in the regular practices of particular groups, in the images and objects people use and to which they refer, and in the organized ways in which they come together and interact. People *act* according to what they think and believe. These acts are not *in consciousness*; they are in what people do, how they insert themselves into a life (in today's tentative idiom, a "life-style"). For it is in living—talking, dancing, driving, eating, dressing, socializing, praying, watching TV—that knowing and believing occur, that they take up a life, that they "get a life."

In the same essay, Althusser emphasized *dominant ideologies*, which are central to the workings of the entire social order and linked to the sectors of the state and the economy. He was concerned with how schools, churches, and courts—the "state apparatuses"—reproduce themselves and the capitalist relations of production and exploitation. Alluding to a letter from Marx to Ludwig Kugelmann, he wrote, "Every child knows that a social formation which did not reproduce the conditions of production at the same time as it produced would not last a year" (1971, p. 127). That is to say, dominant ideologies function in the service of the status quo, keeping classes and institutions in the same relative place, performing the same functions, and adapting to the same prevailing conditions. To accomplish this, ideologies must be believed in by all classes or groups—by the ruling classes themselves and those whose existences they exploit or, perhaps, merely neglect, however systematically. Here, the mystifying features of ideologies come into play: for the ruling classes' ideologies mystify the ruling classes themselves and what they do, just as they mystify those they exploit:

> So when we speak of the class function of an ideology it must be understood that the ruling ideology is indeed the ideology of the ruling class and that the former serves the latter not only in its rule over the exploited class, *but in its own constitution of itself as the ruling class*, by making it accept the lived relation between itself and the world as real and justified.
>
> (Althusser 1969, p. 235)

The theory of ideology as the mystifications of those in power implies that most people in positions of dominance are neither natural cynics nor even well-trained ones. If they were, there would be no need for ideologies—no need to explain or to defend the exploitations that they practice. More important, the persistence of social and political stratification in human societies, and the equally persistent presence of ideologies of the powerful, point to the need of *both* rulers and ruled that inequality be legitimated—a point Althusser stressed in his essay "Marx and Humanism." For ideologies must function for both of these groups and render acceptable to both groups the "reasons" why the structure of power and privilege is so patently lopsided, or at least is so in the present arrangement of things. (The future has always been held out as the "land of promises.") Not surprisingly, these ideologies are cast in what Barrington Moore calls the "language of reciprocity" (1978, pp. 507–9; cf. Eagleton 1991, pp. 27–8), a language that has behind it popular conceptions of justice and injustice, fairness and unfairness. These ideas *legitimate* (literally, make just and righteous) the inequities that exist, while, at the same time, directing the responsibility for these inequities away from those in power:

> Kings call their subjects "my" people, or "our" people. What ruler has ever denied that he had the obligation to serve and protect his or her people? Imperialism finds its justification in the burdens and responsibilities of power to create a more "efficient" division of labor between metropolitan and dependent areas. In general, rulers and dominant groups talk in terms of reciprocity (though they may not use the expression) to stress *their* contribution to the social units they head, and to praise the virtues and necessities of harmonious social relationships therein.
>
> (Moore 1978, p. 508)

While many of these themes bear a close resemblance to the classical uses of the concept of ideology, what distinguishes Althusser's account of it is his notion of how ideologies are formed and sustained and what effects they have, for example: how social divisions are institutionalized in such pivotal social institutions as schools; how the practices of institutions of education operate to "install" people, through "democratic" means, into the existing relations of classes; and how social myths about "equality," "the individual," "equality of opportunity," and "individual achievement" are incorporated into the texts and practices of school programs and national policies of education. Without either disparaging the ideals of American "freedom" and "equality" or reducing them to the status of mere ideologies, the point is that in the face of the inequities that mark United States schools, such ideas are patently ideological. To evoke "freedom" and "equality" in the face of the "savage inequalities" of U.S. schools—to insist that the vast differences in the resources of poor and rich "public" schools are the outcome of conditions whereby economic and political freedoms prevail, whereby families are ultimately responsible for where they live and where their children go to school—is to engage in the *interested* deceits and justifications for which ideologists, whether persons or the "apparatuses" Althusser describes, are notorious. In Jonathan Kozol's book on the inequities of U.S. schools, the lawyer and scholar John Coons describes how such an ideology operates:

> [There is] no graver threat to the capitalist system than the present cyclical replacement of the "fittest" of one generation by their artificially advantaged offspring. Worse, when that advantage is proferred to the children of the successful *by the state*, we can be sure that free enterprise has

40

sold its birthright.... [T]o defend the present public school finance system on a platform of economic or political freedom is no less absurd than to describe it as egalitarian. In the name of all the values of free enterprise, the existing system [is] a scandal.... [W]hat democracy cannot tolerate is an aristocracy padded and protected by the state itself from competition from below.

(Coons in Kozol 1991, pp. 206–7)

Althusser articulates another distinctive theme that has particular relevance for the functions ideologies serve today: ideologies connect people with one another, with a world, and, perhaps most especially, with *themselves*. Ideologies, he claims, are *lived*—they "make allusion to reality." Ideologies bestow identities. For what I know and believe and think are not merely knowledges or beliefs or thoughts; they are what *I* know and what *I* believe and what *I* think. They inscribe themselves in what I do, who I am—my *identity*.

Perhaps it would be useful to individualize Althusser's more general descriptive examples (1971, pp. 166–70) in the following way. If a person believes in God, she goes to church or to temple or to the local assembly. She prays and meets with others who are of her faith. She speaks to her children about God and goodness and faith. There are duties that she knows to be right. These are inscribed in what she does (and doesn't do) when her parents or children get sick, and in what she does for her husband. These actions are given meaning, such as in a community or in an assembly of prayer, in marriage and friendships, and in the feelings that she is allowed to express (or not to express). Her actions are also given meaning in the speeches of churchmen and politicians she listens to about family values and motherhood, in what she is told by those authorities from whom she seeks advice. Then there are the familial, social, and religious rituals attendant upon these actions, providing the occasions where even her bodily gestures express authority in one instance, dependency in another. Then there are the forms and degrees of sentiment attached to these attitudes and ideas. In each of these ways a person's ideas *are* her actions and sentiments and gestures. Her ideas exist in actions; her actions are inserted into *practices*; practices are governed by the rituals she chooses to undergo (Althusser 1971, p. 169).

These three—ideas, practices, and rituals—are "inscribed" within "the *material existence of an ideological apparatus*, be it only a small part of that apparatus: a small mass in a small church, a funeral, a minor match at a sports club, a school day, a political party, etc." (p. 168). Bringing Althusser to the United States today, one's material existence might be manifest at one man's bi-weekly A.A. meeting at the church hall, at one woman's meeting of a lesbian reading group, or at a child's weekly Little League baseball game or Scout meeting. In each of these places ideologies are at work, producing forms of subjectivity, identifying who we are, telling us "that we are indeed concrete, individual, distinguishable and (naturally) irreplaceable subjects," making my me-ness obvious and true: "*all ideology hails or interpellates concrete individuals as concrete individuals . . .*" (pp. 172–3).

IDEOLOGY AS CULTURAL PRACTICE

Despite their differences, we can describe the legacy of both Althusser and Foucault as a theory of ideology as culture: ideologies are neither false nor true, that is, more or less adequate representations of reality; rather, ideologies provide the most fundamental frameworks through which people interpret experience and "live" the conditions available to them. Nor are these frameworks primarily mental, for they exist as *lived practices* of particular groups, classes, communities, and so forth. According to Goran Therborn, who has offered one of the broadest contemporary usages of ideology, ideologies are phenomena of a discursive kind and involve "the constitution and patterning of how human beings live their lives as conscious, reflecting initiators of acts in a structured, meaningful world" (Therborn 1980, p. 15). Thus ideologies do not *distort* as much as they *integrate*, for they are cultural phenomena—systems of representations—that serve to orient human actors to one another and to their worlds. Ideologies circumscribe people's lives, operating as largely unconscious structures that express both how we actually live and how we imagine we live. Ideologies are "an organic part of every social totality. . . . Human societies secrete ideology as the very element and atmosphere indispensable to their historical respiration and life" (Althusser 1969, p. 232). Ideologies operate as *starting points* of arguments and doctrines and positions, as *structures* or categories of thought like those of "the individual" or "family," or "free enterprise" or "choice." Categories and meanings such as these do not reside in Marx's "superstructure" but are primary, that is, "coming before objective things and subjective ideas" (Harland 1987, p. 68).

Yet even if we support (and I do) the contention that ideology's operations are preeminently *cultural*, that is, having to do with the operations of signs, meanings, and discourses, ideology is surely more circumscribed in its effects than "culture," even while its scope has expanded. For ideology specifically involves the relationship between social meanings and power. "Ideology . . . is meaning in the service of power," John B. Thompson writes (1990, p. 7). Something else follows from the theory of ideology as integrative or meaningful: the notion of ideology as the *guardian of identity*.[2] Ideologies "must be 'real' enough to provide the basis on which individuals can fashion a coherent identity, must furnish some solid motivations for effective action, and must make at least some feeble attempt to explain away their own more flagrant contradictions and incoherencies." Ideology, Terry Eagleton contends, "is one crucial way in which the human subject strives to 'suture' contradictions which rive it in its very being, constitute it to the core" (1991, p. 198). It was precisely in this sense that Althusser asserted that ideologies are not so much thought as they are *lived*. Ideologies "can never be purely *instrumental*." Nor are the

42

relations between a ruling ideology and a ruling class "an external and lucid relation of pure utility and cunning." For ideologies situate people, catching them up in their own self-justificatory denouncements and pronouncements about "life," "freedom," "responsibility," "womanhood," and so forth: "a class that *uses* an ideology is its captive too" (Althusser 1969, pp. 234–5).

The *theoretical* importance of Althusser's essay " . . . Ideological State Apparatuses" was undoubtedly his rendering of ideologies as "material practices," the idea contained within the phrase "Ideologies are 'lived.'" More precisely, individuals *"live in ideology* i.e., in a determinate (religious, ethical, etc.) representation of the world" (Althusser 1971, p. 166). For this formulation effectively opened the way for others working on problems of "culture" and cultural "production" and "reproduction" to find a theory compatible with contemporary "suspicions of totality" (Clifford 1988, p. 273). For the contemporary reader, there was something so true in the poststructuralist formulations—rhetorically powerful yet astonishingly tentative—that rendered societies as "unities" only in the sense that they were ideologically *formed*, not given, the outcome of powerful discursive formations (Foucault). "Societies," if they were anything at all, were the effects of the various ideological apparatuses (Althusser)—schools, churches, mass media, sports, and so forth. Cultural and social "totalities" became subject to "exegeses," similar to those that literary and historical texts had undergone. The "text" offered just the right idea on which the new social science could model itself. The legacy of the structuralists, Stuart Hall commented, was its proposal to think of human beings "as spoken by, as well as speaking, their culture: spoken through its codes and systems" (1980, p. 30), an approach that effectively brought "culture" and "ideology" into the minute aspects of the everyday.

Contrary to the viewpoints of some (e.g., Eagleton 1991), this rendering of "culture" and "ideology" as everyday phenomena did not weaken their operations, nor implicitly argue for ideology's end. Rather, it led to a sense of the *discovery* of the operations of power throughout a far more extensive and complex "social formation" (Althusser's term) than had ever before been imagined. Ideology's scope had expanded and its operations turned up in the vast terrain, the diverse sites where culture is produced: modern communication technologies and their institutional settings, artistic centers, scientific organizations and laboratories, schools, government information bureaus, courts, the press, and other vehicles of popular culture. A complex network such as this conjured up and transmitted ideological images, representations, and categories. Ideologies were no longer (had they ever been?) the simple product of a ruling class, the effect of productive forces.

Ideologies, as with all cultural practices, were also "relatively autonomous," irreducible to economic groups and "productive forces." (These, in fact, are not purely "economic" but formations of economic, political, ideological, and theoretical practices.) Their autonomy also meant that ideological practices are *overdetermined*—that economic formations never operate alone but in combina-

43

tion with other elements and forces (Althusser 1969, Part III).[3] "Culture," Stuart Hall explained, "no longer simply reflected other practices in the realm of ideas. It was itself a practice—a *signifying* practice—and had its own determinate product: meaning." For the structuralists and poststructuralists, the "stress therefore shifted from the substantive contents of different cultures to their forms of arrangement—from the *what* to the *how* of cultural systems" (Hall 1980, p. 30). The idea of the primacy of economic forces had given way to a new understanding of the power of representations—sign and symbol. Historical materialist theory, the self-awareness of bourgeois capitalism (Sahlins 1976, p. 166), had given way in this new phase of capitalism's history to a diversity of cultural studies, a phase where commodities' forms had become ineluctably cultural, that is, semiotic (Aronowitz 1990, p. xxv); where knowledge, technique, and the production of symbol and image dominate markets and productive processes; where commodities serve as both sign and carriers of personal and social realities. In this society, even our communities have come to be understood as cultural *imaginings* (Anderson 1991). The self and the body, once thought of as natural objects, have come to be thought of as cultural *projects* (Giddens 1991). In this new phase of modern history and of its academic disciplines and knowledges—a phase distinguished by the primacy and autonomy of all cultural forms—"ideology" has lost its center in "productive forces."

We may, then, speak of ideology's profound "displacement"—an event corresponding to what has been described here as the formidable role of culture and the complex networks in which power, exercised from multiple sites, is strategically produced. This rethinking of ideology has been forced upon us both by this "event" and by theory (the structuralists and poststructuralists). What it is principally about is how to think about ideology as *cultural practice*, that is, as an effect that is cultural and how that effect is linked to particular institutions, groups, and structures. When understood this way, there was something elusive about ideology's operations, something "decentered" about ideology-as-culture (Hall 1992, p. 284). Yet this was precisely what the contemporary understanding of ideology called for: complex inquiries into the connections between cultural forms (knowledges, images, etc.) and institutions, the "discourses" and the "apparatus" in which each is housed.

Proceeding to rethink ideology, we were, after Foucault, trying to think power differently: "Relations of power are not in a position of exteriority with respect to other types of relationships (economic processes, knowledge relationships, sexual relations), but are immanent in the latter" (Foucault 1980a, p. 94). Power is "the multiplicity of force relations immanent in the sphere in which they operate and which constitute their own organization" (p. 92). Accordingly (and this is where these reflections began), social science no longer had "ideology" as its foil, its opposing standard, its justification for itself as knowledge-after-truth. Social science now saw itself as a configuration of the same forces that shaped the landscape of modernity and late modernity. Social science was itself a cultural form and force. Social scientific knowledges describe and are themselves elements of their descriptions.

Foucault's "carceral city," the image with which he ended *Discipline and Punish*, is a description of a new social order, a "new economy of power" (1977, pp. 307–8). This city has neither a "center of power" nor even a "network of forces." In its place, Foucault offers the image of "a multiple network of diverse elements...a strategic distribution of elements of different natures and levels," each mechanism seemingly distinct, but each given over to a new form of rule directed against transgressions of the normal. These are not merely "institutions of repression," although these operate as well, but a series of "'carceral' mechanisms," "rules of strategy," and objects of discourse (medical, sociological, psychiatric, etc.). This is the new material framework—complex and dispersed—in which ideology is housed and in which both the project and the hope of social science are deeply implicated.

The legacy of the structuralist and poststructuralist thinkers, especially Althusser and Foucault, has been a rethinking of power and its operations and manifestations, one from which social science was no longer exempt. However distinctive their views on the legacy of Marxist theory for late modernity, each offered to social theory a vision that burst the confines of ideology's location. Ideology was no longer housed in the bourgeoisie's collective being or in its structures of wealth and labor. Ideology was dispersed throughout a "social order." The concerns of these social theorists were the historical and material existence of ideologies, the connections between knowledges and institutions, and the various fields of knowledge and practice through which power is reproduced, particularly the discourses that regulate and construct what "knowledge" is, how certain systems of thought and their institutional moorings (the state, the university, the medical and legal systems, the scientific estate, etc.)—and not others—are rendered as "knowledge." The theories generated by this group of intellectuals were admittedly complex and diverse and by no means reconcilable in their main features. Yet what they gave social science was the idea of itself as one of the bodies of knowledge, techniques and modes of discourse that configured the modern "subject" and its "society," whose disciplining strategies of observation and objectivity, along with those of medicine, demography, psychology, and education, effectively established the modern standards of normality and the scientific instruments for subjecting these—individual and society—to study.

Given these profound changes in ideology's "social career" (Gouldner 1970), are there sound and even pressing reasons for its use as a concept and a theory for social analysis? This unavoidable question is where Althusser's reading of Marx has taken us, to a place also prepared by Foucault's multiple images of power and its operations. Does "ideology" have a future in the fractured world of late modernity? Can "ideology" play well (or at all) where the holistic (and illusory) vision of one humanity is continually challenged by the prevailing ideas of cultural "difference" and "otherness," and where all truths (and theories) are "local" and partial (see, e.g., Seidman 1991; Lemert 1991)? Yet across this postmodern landscape, ideologists and ideologies still seem to thrive.

In the face of current political and social spectacles, is there not, as Eagleton observes, something absurd in a world "racked by ideological conflict," where "the very notion of ideology has evaporated without trace from the writings of postmodernism and poststructuralism" (1991, p. xi)? If today ideological battles seem more commonplace than special and ideology as familiar as the faces on the evening news, we need to seek out its operations, to relearn (and to teach) how to recognize its forms and its idioms, to discern political interests and the effects they generate.

Admittedly, we can no longer find ideology's operations in the theory of "false consciousness," nor in the affirmation of some great divide between science and ideology. Nor is there anything gained any longer in the idea of true and false knowledges; these usages have become historical moments that should only remain in our collective memory. Yet we can speak today of ideological practices without making the parallel claim that others (such as ourselves) dwell in some realm where only truth and rationality reside.

In fact, today's ideological practices typically wear the garb of rationality or science, or they mask themselves in forms of political practicality (arguments made by Gouldner 1976; Boudon 1989; and Aronowitz 1988). It is also true that today's ideological practices share the perennial strategies—dogmatisms, deceits, and mystifications—that Marx uncovered and which seem deserving of our attention: ideology's lofty voices (we hear them everywhere!) are always authoritative, ruling on the truths and falsehoods of others while passing themselves off as oracles of humanity and the common good. Ideologies still pretend, as Arendt (1968, p. 167) observed, "to know the mysteries of the whole historical process," to assimilate everything and everyone to their own terms and perspectives. Still today, ideologies succeed as ideologies by repressing and by hiding the histories and the circumstances and the strategies from which they derive their own logics; thus Gouldner's claim (1976, p. 48) that the analytic essence of ideology is its "stunted reflexivity" concerning its ideal and material history. Ideology's forgetfulness, if we may call it that, is a strategic and opportunistic amnesia whose will to power is inscribed into its every word and action.

I am not proposing that we continue, as our forebears did, to dream a world-without-ideology; rather, that we grasp the rationality of ideology, a rationality that social theory can, I think, still expose, render problematic, historicize, and oppose. This proposal entails a reading of Marx in light of today's problematics. It is (as our particular postmodern intellectual context has insisted it be) a provisional conception. But—to give the last word to Althusser—"what is not provisional?" (1969, p. 258).

3

THE STRUCTURES OF KNOWLEDGES

The French tradition

[T]he remarkable endeavor of Lévi-Strauss ... appears in the status which he
accords his own discourse on myths ... his discourse on the myth reflects on
itself and criticizes itself. And this moment, this critical period, is evidently of
concern to all the languages which share the field of the human sciences.

(Jacques Derrida)

PRELIMINARY CONSIDERATIONS

The relatively recent discovery of "culture" in social science and social theory is
not only due to the important social transformations of our world in this half
century, changes intensifying our consciousness of cultural phenomena—
"globalization," the rise of a postindustrial society and its information
technologies, the growing consciousness of world peoples about one another.
Today's "cultural turn"[1] is also a response to mid- and late-twentieth-century
intellectual movements, particularly the sciences of linguistics and semiotics,
whose impact has extended to fields as wide-ranging as literary studies and
psychoanalysis, sociology and anthropology. More than any other figure
working in the social sciences, the work of Claude Lévi-Strauss, whose
"structural anthropology" was inspired by the structural linguistics of
Ferdinand de Saussure, has forced upon us a rethinking about the operations
of language and of collective symbols and myths.

It is the *logic* or form of reasoning of structuralism that has guided our
current rethinking in social science about the linguistic features of all social
phenomena; it was Lévi-Strauss whose work advanced the extraordinary
proposition that *all* social forms follow language rules—language and cultural
phenomena are homologous.[2] Regardless of where one stands relative to this
proposition, the argument that all social phenomena serve as parts of a system
of signification has altered the way we now see human societies.

In this chapter (as in Chapter 2 on Marxism and Chapter 4 on American
pragmatism), the tradition of French sociology is described as a body of work of
vital importance for the sociology of knowledge. Its distinct vision is that of the
power and force of collective ideas and sentiments. It extends from Emile

47

Durkheim's claims concerning how collective consciousness is derived from the forms of social organization and the division of labor and how collective ideas are symbolic representations of social experiences, to other works on the primacy of collective categories (Mauss, Bloch, Granet, Lévi-Strauss). The work of Lévi-Strauss is not only continuous with that of Durkheim in many respects but also supersedes it, particularly in its claim that there is always an underlying structure (or hidden relations) that renders the disorderly and incoherent domain of culture coherent and orderly: *culture is structured* and every social form is a potential sign.

For sociology, even more far-reaching in its impact is Lévi-Strauss's argument that his own analysis of myth is itself a part of the system of myths that he analyzes. Lévi-Strauss offers us a vision of Western civilized peoples and their sciences (ethnography, ethnology) as *cultural* projects (albeit rational ones), built up in much the same way that the "savages" build up their worlds—through systems of classification that establish difference and otherness. Western knowledges, including scientific ones, are neither primarily nor exclusively concerned with objective representations of reality. As cultural projects, Western knowledges express, interpret, and communicate, and they do so principally through distinctions and oppositions (Lévi-Strauss 1966a, p. 268). This they have in common with all systems of myth. Structuralism is an ethnography of *all of us*.

STRUCTURALISM: FROM DURKHEIM TO LÉVI-STRAUSS

It was Durkheim who advanced the first "structuralist" claim that religion—"the most primitive of all social phenomena"—provided the key for unlocking all other collective activities: law, morality, art, science, and so forth. Indeed, all of social life, he reasoned, could be explained "not by the conception of it formed by those who participate in it, but by the profound causes which escape their consciousness," particularly the powerful effects of collective symbols and *représentations* in the creation of a society (Durkheim [1897] 1982, pp. 171–3). While he attributed a special importance to the economic realm and its effects and to the ways people organize themselves into groups, his position, particularly at the time of writing *The Rules of Sociological Method* and after, was of the "preponderance of religion" (Lukes 1972, p. 233): religion is "the system of symbols by means of which society becomes conscious of itself (Durkheim [1897] 1951, p. 312); it is the source of all forms of thought and leaves its imprint upon later philosophies of nature, including scientific ones. Furthermore, Durkheim argued that collective ideas or representations—the various ways a people re-present their collective experience of life-in-common—take on an autonomous function in relation to the group itself ([1914] 1983, p. 85); communal life itself "presupposes common ideas." And while it is collective existence and the ideas and representations that are generated out of that existence that become palpable truths for those who live it, "in the last analysis, it is thought which creates reality." Thought's preeminent creation is *society* itself ([1914] 1983, p. 85).

The structuralist quality to Durkheim's reasoning is also found in his argument, consciously set against the theories of the American pragmatist philosophers (Durkheim [1914] 1983), that representation is a collective accomplishment. It is precisely its collective source that gives to these ideas their force, their truth, and their appearance of objectivity. He described social life "as the mother and eternal nurse of moral thought and logical thinking, of science as well as faith" (Lévi-Strauss 1945, p. 530).

The persistence and force of the collective categories run through all of Durkheim's inquiries. Even in his early positivist treatise *The Division of Labor in Society*, it was the *collective idea of the individual*, a product of social development, that both expressed the market relationships of the new industrial economy and was capable of altering its moral basis. Individualism is a set of moral, indeed, *religious* ideas: as with all other beliefs, "moral individualism" derives its force from society ([1893] 1933, Ch. 5).

The theme of the primacy of collective symbols and images is, of course, older than Durkheim, and its lineage is decidedly "French." Indeed, the study of mental operations (*mentalités*), particularly "linguistic habits" and their collective manifestations, is identified with the leading figures of modern French intellectual history and contributors to the different fields of *les sciences de l'homme*. The philosophical and moral concerns of its early formulators, Condorcet, Montesquieu, Rousseau, and Comte, were recast by Durkheim into social scientific terms. Durkheim's program of treating symbols and images as social phenomena—as objects and events in nature—and his proposal that sociology be "objective, specific, and methodical" ([1901] 1982, p. 35) were continued by Marcel Granet writing on Chinese language and culture, Lucien Levy-Bruhl on the primitive mind, Maurice Halbwachs on collective memory, and Marcel Mauss on classification and social categories. Mauss ([1938] 1979, p. 22) described the collective symbol as "an invoked genie" that had "a life of its own; it acts and reproduces itself indefinitely." Durkheim argued that a society's *représentations collectives* were so fundamental to thinking that our logical categories of time and space, for example, were socially derived, "closely connected with the corresponding social organization" (Durkheim and Mauss 1963, p. 88).

There has been, then, a peculiarly French proclivity for describing the operations of language and collective symbolism. Because of it, one can observe in Durkheim's reasoning or "methodology" concerns that anticipate those of the contemporary structuralists Lévi-Strauss, Jacques Lacan, and Roland Barthes. For example, Durkheim's important and late treatise *The Elementary Forms of the Religious Life* employs a mode of reasoning whereby religious phenomena (rituals, gods, iconography, etc.) are true insofar as they express the social conditions that generate them. One must know, Durkheim reasons, how to bore beneath "the [religious] symbol to the reality which it represents and which gives it its meaning" (1915, p. 2), to seek out the origins of a society's categories in the forms of social life itself. Durkheim's sense is not that social myths and categories are housed in a single underlying domain, as Marx argued about the primacy of "material life," but that languages, especially the powerful collective myths of a people, are used to understand the operations of the various and different social phenomena—its kinship and marriage systems, and so forth—that characterize a social group or society. Structuralism's reasoning (recognizable, but unsustained in Durkheim's own writings) is that *all* social forms and activities follow "the same set of abstract rules that define and govern what we normally think of as a language" (Lane 1970, p. 14). As early as Mauss's *Essai sur le don* of 1924, Lévi-Strauss ([1950] 1968) tells us, the structuralist proposition was advanced that kinship relations, relations of economic exchange, and linguistic relations are of the same order, thereby opening the way for linguistic theory to be applied to the realm of social facts and to inquire into the underlying laws by which these "signs" take their meaning.

In his extended "Introduction" to structuralist methods in disciplines as diverse as literary criticism and mathematics, Michael Lane (1970, p. 14) observes how structuralists apply linguistic theory to objects and activities outside of language itself:

> In an attempt to reduce terminological confusion the word "code" is sometimes used, notably by Roland Barthes, to cover all types of socially employed systems of communication. All these social codes are seen to have, like natural languages, a lexicon, or "vocabulary." If we take as an example the code of kinship and marriage, as Lévi-Strauss did in his first major book (. . . *Elementary Structures of Kinship*), we see that all those members of a society who stand in a kinship relation (or kinship relations) to other members constitute the lexicon, or repertory, of permissable terms. The rules about who may, and who may not, marry whom, constitute the syntax or grammar, which determines what elements may be legitimately (or "meaningfully") strung together. Roland Barthes has similarly attempted (in *Système de la mode*) to construct a lexicon and syntax for fashion.

Any and all social forms can, in principle, be subjected to a structuralist analysis, in the sense that "text," "language," and "myth" have been broadly and unexpectedly applied to "extra-linguistic languages" (Sontag's term, 1968)—for example, to totemism, to practices of kinship and cooking, to categories of food (Lévi-Strauss), or to fashion, or the spectacle of wrestling, or even to the meanings of eating steak or using detergents (Barthes). Accordingly, myths are not descriptive but serve as "models for description (or thinking)—according to the formula of Lévi-Strauss logical techniques for resolving basic antinomies in thought and social existence" (Sontag 1968,

p. xx). The "myths" of Lévi-Strauss, say, or the "codes" of Barthes serve as techniques for burrowing beneath the ordinary perception of things where various social forms become *things to think with* (Darnton 1984): they can be broken down to their underlying logics, and their ways of organizing and classifying reality revealed. Structuralist methods are based on the notion that human beings use whatever is at their disposal—stories, movies, fashion, sports, food—to render their worlds and themselves meaningful and to communicate important messages. Based on this premise of the communicational aspects of things, the structuralists use totems and fairy tales or myths about war or about women to examine what these things (*les choses*) communicate and signal (e.g., What are the logics of myths, marriage rules, kinship systems, totems, etc.?). These "things," as Durkheim described the realm of "social facts" ([1901] 1982), are used to make visible a society's "deeper reality"—reason (*esprit*) that operates unconsciously and underlies all social phenomena.[3] "Both marriage systems and mythic systems are about proper communication," observes James Boon,

> a kind of combined ethics and aesthetics—balanced against certain threats and risks. The ultimate threat against orderly communication is non-circulation (incest in the realm of social exchange; silence or non-questions and non-answers in the realm of language).
>
> (1985, p. 165)

Structuralism "is a method whose primary intention is to permit the investigator to go beyond a pure description of what he perceives or experiences (*le vécu*)" (Lane 1970, p. 31). The case will be made here that structuralist methods surely belie a late-twentieth-century (postmodern) preoccupation with language and communication. However, structuralist inquiries also participate in a distinctly modern penchant for "disenchantment": from Durkheim's argument (Freud's, too) that rational thought is built upon unconscious operations, to Lévi-Strauss's search for the "meaningful" at the level below the surface of the consciously rational.

Marxism, geology, and psychoanalysis, Lévi-Strauss's *trois maîtresses* as he referred to them, instructed him in the deception of appearances: "All three [Freud, Marx, geology] demonstrate that understanding consists in reducing one type of reality to another; that the true reality is never the most obvious; and that the nature of truth is already indicated by the care that it takes to remain elusive" (Lévi-Strauss [1955] 1977, p. 50). The reality of the psychological, the social, the physical springs from a common source. This source, at the same time, "irrigates" the surface world, conferring upon it intelligibility.

Social forms play on the observer's eye like a landscape, appearing as a "vast chaos" of disparate, unconnected elements; however, as one knows the geological history of a terrain, its "unconscious life" if we may call it that, a master-meaning emerges, of which the elements are but partial or distorted transpositions (Lévi-Strauss [1955] 1977, p. 48). In both cases, that of psychoanalysis and geology, seeing is neither believing nor really seeing, since the objects of both are opaque:

> In both cases, the researcher, to begin with, finds himself faced with seemingly impenetrable phenomena: in both cases, in order to take stock of, and gauge, the elements of a complex situation, he must display subtle qualities, such as sensitivity, intuition and taste. And yet, the order which is thus introduced into a seemingly incoherent mass is neither contingent nor arbitrary. Unlike the history of the historians, that of the geologist is similar to the history of the psychoanalyst in that it tries to project in time—rather in the manner of a *tableau vivant*—certain basic characteristics of the physical or mental universe.
>
> (Lévi-Strauss [1955] 1977, p. 49)

In the realm of social phenomena, Lévi-Strauss claims to have learned a similar lesson from Marx. Social science is no more founded "on the basis of events than physics is founded on sense data" ([1955] 1977, p. 50). Rather, its aim is to construct theoretic models to be rigorously tested and studied, from which conclusions can be formed to interpret empirical phenomena. In *Structural Anthropology*, Marx is explicitly claimed as an apostle of structuralism, who strove to "uncover the symbolic systems which underlie both language and man's relationship with the universe" (Lévi-Strauss 1963, p. 95).

The system of language

Lévi-Strauss acknowledges his indebtedness to the twentieth-century science of linguistics (this is also a feature of the structuralist approaches in literature and psychoanalysis), particularly methods centered around the problem of the *sign* as developed by three sources: first and most important, the seminal work of Ferdinand de Saussure (1966), his lectures delivered between 1906 and 1911 and first published in 1959 as *Course of General Linguistics*; second, the work of the Russian Formalists, particularly the structural linguist Roman Jakobson; third, the work of the Prague Linguistic Circle (and their "phonological" approach to language) in the years 1926 to 1939.

Saussure's work, particularly his view of language (*la langue*) as a collective phenomenon and a social institution that is coherent and orderly—a self-regulating object of inquiry distinct from speech (*la parole*)—opened up an entire intellectual movement that sought to examine how this structure or system of language operated. The idea of language as a system of signs is Saussure's principal legacy.

In the most general terms, structuralism takes as its project the study of the elements of language (or signs), arguing that these elements or signs take their value or meaning from their relationships to other signs. The language–speech distinction has proved important not only because it proposed that language (*la langue*) operates *as a system*, but also because it has opened up a form of reasoning whereby individual variants of a "language" or code, such as a myth, could be used to reveal the underlying logic of the entire (mythic) system. For just as through speech one can gain access to the underlying structure of language, "apparent structures" of other kinds (mythic, psychological, literary) provide entrance into the study of underlying structures or total fields or systems of communication (Poole 1969, pp. 10–11). To take another instance, kinship or totemic systems operate (as with other "languages") according to syntactical rules of opposition and interdependence and reveal "messages" or forms of communication taking place between social groups (Benoist 1978, p. 4).

For Lévi-Strauss (1963, p. 20), structural linguistics, turning in the direction of phonology and phonemic analysis, revolutionized linguistic science (and anthropology at the same time). The linguistic elements that are analyzed are no longer signs (words) but minimal units of sound, *phonemes*, which are at the deepest level of human speech; these constitute the unconscious infrastructure of language.

According to the linguistic model of the Prague school as developed by Jakobson, all phonemic systems are described in terms of a single and small set of some twelve or more kinds of binary oppositions.[4] Everything else is elaboration and combination, reflecting unconscious structure at every level of reality. The laws of linguistics formulate necessary relationships, describing the fundamental structure of language; through language, which is coextensive with human culture and which is humankind's primary mode of symbolization, one may look into the deepest structure of the human mind. Modern linguistics, then, provides Lévi-Strauss with a scientific tool for burrowing beneath appearances to the unconscious, invariable, universal structure of the human mind. Now it is only for him to transpose the linguistic model to any of humankind's cultural products (whether kinship systems, cuisine, or myths) for his enterprise to get underway. In the case of marriage rules and kinship systems, for example, one can observe types of *communication* at work:

> That the mediating factor, in this case, should be the *women of the group*, who are *circulated* between clans, lineages, or families, in place of the *words of the group*, which are *circulated* between individuals, does not at all change the fact that the essential aspect of the phenomenon is identical in both cases.
>
> (Lévi-Strauss 1963, p. 61)

The "identity" of the social practices and utterances, in this example, derives from the fact that "both sets of performances, the linguistic and the social, are regulated by codes or laws which underlie them; and in the fact that they are regulated by a syntactical matrix" (Benoist 1978, p. 66).

Structuralism's focus on "structures" gives priority to the whole over its parts:[5] "the system of interconnections among all aspects of social life plays a more important part in the transmission of culture than any one of those aspects considered separately" (Lévi-Strauss 1963, p. 358). According to this linguistic logic, language is a system of signs studied "synchronically," that is, as a total system at a given point in time, and where not the elements, but the whole is studied, particularly the network of relations that unite the elements. The meaning or sense of the elements is derived only from a study of their interrelations, and of the location of an element within a set. Or, the value of a linguistic sign depends upon its relationship to a total vocabulary. According to this logic, Lévi-Strauss argues that the many and diverse hunting and creation myths, Amazonian and North American, form a unified system ("vocabulary"), and that all the variants of these myths actually constitute a unified pattern—"that the sum of related tales is a living aggregate, a code of cultural reinterpretation in which single elements are regrouped but not lost" (Steiner 1967, p. 248). In Lévi-Strauss's "The Structural Study of Myth," he reminds us that all the variants of a myth need to be considered for a successful analysis; if, for example, one were studying the Oedipus myth, Freud's interpretation would have to be included as a variant of the set (Lévi-Strauss 1963, p. 217). So his coding of the codes of myth is itself a "myth of mythology" ([1962] 1969, p. 12).

Lévi-Strauss's myth analysis proceeds by way of his linguistic model. Myth, a part of human speech, is both language (*la langue*) and more than language. Encompassing as it does the elements of speaking (*la parole*), myth manifests its uniqueness at a third level, which contains the two. Myth at once embraces the "structural side of language" (*la langue*) and its "statistical aspect" (*la parole*) (Lévi-Strauss 1963, pp. 209–10). Defined in terms of synchrony and diachrony, mythic time is at once reversible (which belongs to *la langue*) and irreversible (which belongs to *la parole*): "a myth always refers to events alleged to have taken place long ago. But what gives myth an operational value is that the specific pattern described is timeless: it explains the present and the past as well as the future" (1963, p. 209). It appears that it is the diachronic referent of myth (narrative) that supplies Lévi-Strauss with the matrices of meaning, the constitutive units of myth—"mythemes." These mythemes, like phonemes, are not isolated relations but "bundles of such relations" (1963, p. 211), which may be grouped on a synchronic axis of difference and opposition. It is this last arrangement that allows the mythemes to be read as a virtually endless chain of relations both to other mythemes and to other myths. What finally is the meaning of all these matrices of meaning? In *The Raw and the Cooked*, the "final meaning" of mythological thought is addressed this way:

> [M]yths signify the mind that evolves them by making use of the world of which it is itself a part. Thus there is simultaneous production of myths themselves, by the mind that generates them and, by the myths, of an image of the world which is already inherent in the structure of the mind.... By taking its raw material from nature, mythic thought proceeds in the same way as language, which chooses phonemes from

among the natural sounds of which a practically unlimited range is to be found in childish babbling . . . the material is the instrument of meaning, not its object. For it to play this part, it must be whittled down. Only a few of its elements are retained—those suitable for the expression of contrasts or forming pairs of opposites.

(Lévi-Strauss [1964] 1969, p. 341)

MYTHS AND MINDS: A NEW VISION OF CULTURE

The difficult passage above by Lévi-Strauss contains a number of startling claims—revolutionary, actually, with respect to the enterprise of social science and its objects of study. For Lévi-Strauss's reflection on the "final meaning" of mythological thought is also a reflection on its own status as *knowledge*. As early as *Totemism* ([1962] 1969), Lévi-Strauss advanced the claim—thereby superseding Durkheim's *Elementary Forms* (1915)—that the project of the human sciences, an instance of Western rational discourse, was only one variation in the entire field of human knowledge. Furthermore (and this is why it so thoroughly repositions the sociology of knowledge), the discourse of his own anthropological study of myths (his "mythologicals") is treated as a system of signification existing alongside and within other mythic systems.

A brief excursion into the text of Lévi-Strauss's *Totemism* reveals it as a work that both marked the beginning of the expansion of structuralism in France and served as an introduction to *The Savage Mind* (1966a). Totemic systems and practices, which were for Durkheim (and for McLennan, Frazer, Robertson Smith, Tylor, and Malinowski) substantive things requiring explanation, were approached (by Lévi-Strauss) as *signifying systems* in need of interpretation. Totemic systems are not historically and socially distinct phenomena as much as they are systems that tell us how *all* human minds categorize and communicate. In the passage cited above (see pp. 54–5) from *The Raw and the Cooked*, totemic myths—as with all myths—"signify the minds that evolve them." Myths (and totems) show us how minds draw from nature and how (as in the case of language) the categories that minds construe (raw/cooked, man/ woman, living/dead, eaglehawk/crow, bat/night owl . . .) serve as conceptual tools for saying things and for elaborating abstract ideas. Totemic classifications serve as complex and many-layered significations. Totemic creatures (e.g., the classifications of eagles according to type, color, and stage of life) operate not as creatures themselves, but as things for the Osage to think with; eagles provide "conceptual tools." "We do not believe," a member of the Osage tribe explains, "that our ancestors were really animals, birds, etc. as told in traditions. These things are only . . . [symbols] of something higher" (Dorsey cited in Lévi-Strauss 1966a, p. 149). Totemic classifications also serve to "divide men up from each other." For totemic symbols are borrowed from nature to erase the obvious resemblances human beings share and to assert their differences and divisions (Poole 1969, p. 62; cf. Lévi-Strauss 1966a, p. 62).

Totemism opens with a discussion of the "illusion of totemism," that is, of treating totemism as a phenomenon in its own right. The argument is advanced that totemism *signifies*, rather than reveals, a thing in need of explanation, along with the claim that the various *theories* about totemism also need to be swept into the very problem that totemism opened up. By fitting together "savage minds" and "civilized logics," the work is as much a systematic reflection on how we ("normal, white adult men," in Lévi-Strauss's words) construe primitives and savages (and ourselves), as it is a study of totemic signs. For, after all, totemic myths (like all myths) are "in-terminable" (Lévi-Strauss [1962] 1969, p. 6) and include all their variants (whether from peoples of the bush who practice totemism or from moderns who use "totemism" to think with).

"Totemism is like hysteria," the book opens. Both are contemporary phenomena,

> arising from the same cultural conditions, and their parallel misadventures may be initially explained by a tendency, common to many branches of learning towards the close of the nineteenth century, to mark off certain human phenomena—as though they constituted a natural entity—which scholars preferred to regard as alien to their own moral universe, thus protecting the attachment which they felt towards the latter.
>
> (Lévi-Strauss [1962] 1969, p. 69)

Totemism isn't really about totemism, if we mean by that the religious practices of primitive peoples involving animals or plants as sacred objects. What is interesting and compelling about totemic phenomena is what signifying power the various elements of a totemic system or totemic code have for the people themselves, as well as for those of us who construe something about others and ourselves in the process. Lévi-Strauss alluded to the problem of totemism earlier, in his 1960 inaugural address at the Collège de France, as "transparent and insubstantial"—its importance in anthropological thinking stemmed "from a certain taste for the obscene and the grotesque . . . a negative projection of an uncontrollable fear of the sacred." The theory of totemism was "developed 'for us' (*pour nous*) and not 'in itself' (*en soi*). Nothing guarantees that, in its current form, it does not still proceed from a similar illusion" (1976, p. 27).

Among the many vitally important effects of Lévi-Strauss's structuralism, which it shares with some other late-twentieth-century methods subsumed under the rubric of "literary theory" or theories of the "text," is that (perhaps, despite itself) it draws attention to itself as a particular kind of text with a *con*text; it is a work written by a citizen of "civilization," the text itself a part of "culture" and "cultural production," and, by implication, a part of "ruling"

(Gramsci) or "governing" (Foucault), processes seen today as eminently *cultural*. Unlike earlier proponents of social science, today's theories of culture place their own enterprise smack in the middle of the cultural domain that they study, "producing works of ourselves and against ourselves" (Boon 1985, p. 163). "Texts are worldly," Edward Said asserts, adding (contra Lévi-Strauss) "to some degree they are events, and even when they appear to deny it, they are nevertheless a part of the social world" (Said 1983, p. 4). Or, to cite a contemporary anthropologist, "The study of culture *is* culture . . . *our* culture; it operates through our forms, creates in our terms, borrows our words and concepts for its meanings, and re-creates us through our efforts" (Wagner 1981, p. 16).

This acute sense that "knowledge" and "culture" are produced in and through (and not outside of) the confrontations of world peoples and powers has arisen today at a time when virtually all world peoples are implicated in one way or another in each other's "culture," when there are no longer any "pure" cultures, and among peoples whose lives (and cultures) are profoundly implicated in each others' lives (and cultures). Today, especially, Lévi-Strauss observes, the diversity of cultures "is less a function of the isolation of groups than of the relationships which unite them" (Lévi-Strauss 1976, p. 328). "Authentic human differences are disintegrating" (Clifford 1988, p. 14).

How disconcerting, then, that at precisely this time, "multiculturalist" voices assert the contrary and insist on the "recognition" and expression of an "authentic" cultural identity and heritage (Taylor *et al.* 1994)—at a moment when culturally distinct peoples hardly exist any more. Perhaps "multi-culturalism"—like a cultural slight-of-hand—expresses this "recognition" of the disappearance of distinct and authentic cultures and, in the face of this disappearance, the need to create communities and cultures. Multiculturalism may, then, be about cultural survival in a climate of confrontation (Appiah 1994). Multiculturalism, as with other *isms* such as nationalism, operates as a unifying and totalizing *myth* of culture and its location (Bhabha 1994).

Some anthropologists have referred to the project of anthropological study at century's end as the "predicament of culture" (Clifford 1988; cf. Clifford and Marcus 1986; Marcus and Fischer 1986; Geertz 1995), with its distinctly ironic sense of what it means to be "writing culture" or writing about culture, an irony that effectively undermines the enterprise of ethnography as it is underway. In the works of Lévi-Strauss, the responses to this contemporary condition have ranged from world-weariness, to resignation, to sharp critique, such as in his treatment of the art of writing as a principal means for the facilitation of slavery (Lévi-Strauss [1955] 1977, p. 338). Yet this particular vision of one's place among world peoples—a panoply, at once disturbing and overwhelming, with images of difference and incongruity—also evokes a peculiarly humane vision (distinct from liberalism's confident and progressive "humanism"). For it is through an understanding of the "savage mind" (through which we may see nature more clearly) that we can grasp better what we are. Cultures are, after all, diachronic accessories to synchronic structures. Modern societies, having spawned bigger and more elaborate and vastly complex human institutions, have obscured their relation to the mystery of being which resides in the heart of matter—or in the "brief glance . . . one can sometimes exchange with a cat" (Lévi-Strauss [1955] 1977, p. 474).

Structural anthropology's claim is that a people's "culture" is principally deciphered in and through its signifying systems—whether its languages (in the literal sense) or its other modes of communicating through objects and others—and through the categories and classifications in which these are construed. Cultural operations—and they are many things, reducible neither to "material life" nor to symbols floating in air—are systems of evaluation and discrimination. What a society or people *is*, therefore, is what it says and believes it is *not*. Cultural operations *differentiate* in nearly endless ways, as both Lévi-Strauss and Foucault have (differently) shown us. Edward Said's work (which exists in Foucault's vicinity more than in Lévi-Strauss's) addresses the precise ways that the notion of culture is inextricably tied to the "notion of place" and that of boundaries:

> I shall use the word *culture* to suggest an environment, process, and hegemony in which individuals . . . and their works are embedded . . . culture is used to designate not merely something to which one belongs but something that one possesses and, along with that proprietary process, culture also designates a boundary by which the concepts of what is extrinsic or intrinsic to the culture come into forceful play.
>
> (Said 1983, pp. 8–9)

As Lévi-Strauss himself has observed, assuming his stance as classic *moraliste*, the designations and discriminations, the categories and classifications of Western peoples—carried in our theories of race and culture, in our philosophy and our biology—are the distinctions of ours and theirs, of civilized and savage, oppositions for shoring up national identities and histories. In *The Savage Mind*, he explicitly and systematically opposes the primitive and civilized distinction, which is founded upon the notion of a development of the human mind from inferior to superior stages. The distinction between primitive and modern, or between magic and science, is rather the result of specific options taken by the human mind in its relation to its environment. Primitive science (the "science of the concrete"), though restricted by its essence, is no less "scientific" and no less genuine than the exact natural sciences (Lévi-Strauss 1966a, p. 16).

Lévi-Strauss is no sociologist of knowledge, at least not in the usual sense. Yet there is a "subtext" to his work, captured in an unforgettable phrase, at least for those social scientists who regularly wrestle with the problem of the ideological and unconscious operations of knowledges: "the nature of truth is already indicated by the care that it takes to remain elusive" ([1955] 1977, p. 50). *The care that it takes to remain elusive is a mark of its truthfulness*; or, as

Lévi-Strauss writes in *The Way of Masks*, "Like a myth, a mask denies as much as it affirms. It is not made solely of what it says or thinks it is saying, but of what it excludes" (1982, p. 144). There is significance (truth) in what societies assert as well as in what they deny or suppress. This position is neither Freudian nor Marxist in intent, that is, arguing for the discovery of a real underlying structure that reveals the truths behind the realm of false appearances. Nor is Lévi-Strauss's "care that it takes to remain elusive" a statement about unconscious motivations. (Lévi-Strauss, after Saussure, asserted the nonmotivation of the symbolic function.) Rather, it is a statement about the various levels on which the human mind operates: cultural forms, *as culture*, render themselves and their operations invisible through a process of conversions and transformations seen in the diverse forms of myths and other social forms and practices. What these transformations "reveal" (by concealing) is the total range of their meanings and messages. In the realm of culture, the science of human artifacts (myths, stories, images, etc.) asks not only what these things represent, but what they choose *not* to represent (Boon 1985, pp. 162–3).

This notion of meaning through concealment evokes Foucault's accounts of "cultural exclusions," namely, how certain "alterities," or "others," have been silenced or rendered invisible by penal disciplines and repressive (sexual) discourses. The similarity is more than apparent. Both Lévi-Strauss and Foucault propose a dialectic of cultural operations where meanings emerge through a process of differentiations: self/other, normal/pervert, sane/mad. In Said's terms,

> culture achieves its hegemony over society and the State ... based on a constantly practiced differentiation of itself from what it believes to be not itself. And this differentiation is frequently performed by setting the valorized culture over the Other ... culture often has to do with an aggressive sense of nation, home, community, and belonging.
>
> (Said 1983, p. 12).

Despite his lack of preoccupation with power and its discursive operations, Lévi-Strauss shares with his contemporaries their "cultural relativity": every culture is equivalent to every other culture; the logics of the civilized mind have no higher place in the annals of humankind than those of the savages—"a good deal of egocentricity and naivety is necessary to believe that man has taken refuge in a single one of the historical or geographical modes of his existence, when the truth about man resides in the system of their differences and common properties" (Lévi-Strauss 1966a, p. 249). In this respect, his image of *bricolage* is instructive.

The *bricoleur* is a kind of an odd-job man shaping new things out of old with material that is "at hand." The repertory of his materials is limited and varied—things that were parts of other things and which, therefore, themselves preconstrain the shapes of new constructs. Creative readaptation and rearrangement characterize his activity. Unlike the engineer, he does not build with materials specifically designed for his purpose. Mythic thought, then, is a kind of *bricolage* of the human mind, which builds its institutions from the debris of previous ones, rearranging past constructions and destructions. It seeks always to reinstitute its fragile stability, forming structures from the remains of events. Like language (in the Saussurean distinction), mythic thought, essentially synchronic in nature, is particularly susceptible to the influence of diachrony. Inversely, modern science "creates its means and results in the form of events, thanks to the structures which it is constantly elaborating and which are its hypotheses and theories" (Lévi-Strauss 1966a, p. 22). Again, for Lévi-Strauss, the approach of each differs. Modern thought may be able to disregard some of the results of mythic *bricolage* but not the validity of its original option. It was, after all, the option of a form of thought that discovered agriculture, animal domestication, and pottery—the basis of a revolution, the neolithic revolution, which, for Lévi-Strauss, compares more than favorably with the consequent developments of humankind.

Perceived in terms of history, the distinction between "primitive" and "modern" further translates the terms of these options. Lévi-Strauss prefers to classify societies as "hot" or "cold" (1968, p. 46). "Hot" societies (modern), having internalized the historic process, make it the moving power of their development with ever-accelerating releases of energy, fueled by their sharp differentiations between "power and opposition, majority and minority, exploiter and exploited . . . between castes and between classes," differences and exploitations "urged unceasingly in order to extract social change and energy from them": "historical development at the price of the transformation of [human beings] into machines" (1968, pp. 47–8). It is not that "cold" societies (primitive) are without history, but rather they "seem to have elaborated or retained a particular wisdom which incites them to resist desperately any structural modification that would afford history a point of entry into their lives" (1968, p. 48). Their institutions are particularly suited to annul or neutralize change, to absorb events into structures, to suppress time.

Whither/whether structuralism?

As a movement of the 1950s and early 1970s, structuralism, to speak in simple and unitary terms about a complex movement, has been described by some of its principal commentators as "a moving target" (Lemert 1990, p. 231) and as a movement that has already been routinized into "texts" (Kurzweil 1980)— texts that have served to open up new projects and *isms*, such as poststructuralism and postmodernism. Beginning with Lévi-Strauss's (1968) early claim to decipher "the unconscious nature of collective phenomena," on to Althusser's rereading of Marx and its/his "destruction" of Marxist humanism (Althusser 1969), and then to Barthes's structuralist essays on literature and writing (Barthes [1953] 1968), it is a movement that has not met its own scientific promises to uncover deep unconscious mental operations. Yet, in other respects, the movement has religiously obeyed its principal claim that culture is a *system of differences*, whereby the meaning of a single unit is defined through a system of oppositions with other units. By this logic—a logic that, *inter alia*, offered a theory of the "autonomy of culture"—the structuralists opened the way for themselves to be superseded. As Derrida was probably the first to point out, and in terms that set into motion the era of poststructuralism and postmodernism, structuralist propositions and methods opened up the logic that "everything [is] discourse" (Derrida 1970, p. 249): structuralism's "discourse on 'structure,'" its critique of language, insists that "language bears within itself the necessity of its own critique" and insists that its own discourse on myths exists among the other "mythologicals." Lévi-Strauss's structuralism "was its own gravedigger" (Lemert 1990, p. 233). Or, using anthropology's notion of culture-as-invention (Wagner 1981), the age of structuralism represented a particular stage in Western intellectuals' own cultural awareness, a moment when the "human" was being reinvented and when the presence of the "subject" of the modern age had begun to be displaced by the operations of languages and myths that were thought to invent "society," "Man," or "nature" itself.

By now, structuralism has been scrutinized both as incapable of living up to its scientific claims and, from postmodernism's position, as continuing to track in on its boots traces of the dried mud of modernist humanism and ethnocentrism. From another point of view, structuralism really did itself in when it decided to take language seriously (and the user's language less seriously). Doing this it unseated ("decentered") the "subject" and undermined the status of reality as well, undoing its own claim to establish a science of universal mental operations (Best and Kellner 1991).

Structuralism's most consequential claim—one that is inscribed in the theories of those who have superseded it—is its disregard (following Saussure) of things-in-themselves, or the relationship between words and things. Structuralism's view of language is one of a *structure* of signifying relations between signifiers and signifieds, words and concepts, rather than between words and things. It disregards or brackets any concern with representation, taking up instead the interminable process of signifiers and signifieds. This it shares, for better or worse depending on one's temperament and allegiances, with poststructuralism and postmodernism (Hutcheon 1988, pp. 148–9).

But what does this imply for those of us who still stand as social scientists in the shadow of Durkheim? Must we today, along with Lévi-Strauss, each declare ourselves Durkheim's "inconstant disciple" (Durkheim and Mauss 1963, Dedication)? Has Durkheim, in some final sense, been superseded? These questions, as I argued in Chapter 1, are concerned with the problem of revisiting or rereading the classics in the light of our time, as well as reading them within the new perspectives and problems that characterize "contemporary thought"—a wholistic notion, but one that may serve as a means to organize and identify common features of disparate thinkers and texts. In a time when "authentic human differences are disintegrating" (Clifford 1988, p. 14), I'll risk offending current fashion by invoking the idea of commonality. Besides, it is appropriately Durkheimian.

Returning to the questions raised above, we need not choose Lévi-Strauss over Durkheim (or vice versa). If anything is a mark of our times and our particular perspectives, it is the realization that today's categories, and the insights that they afford us, allow us to create a truly *syncretist sociology*, characterized by "the mingling of strange gods . . . or the melange of cultural artifacts . . . the jumbling" of aesthetic styles and perspectives. Daniel Bell (1976, p. 13) used this term to describe a distinct feature of modern culture and its free style to make itself up in a manner much like the modern self's need to achieve "self-realization." It is appropriately descriptive of our option today as social scientists and social theorists.

Accordingly, the study of cultural formations and practices views them as many things: as expressive and representational (Lévi-Strauss), as sharing an underlying or "deep structure," and as open to a "world"—as Durkheim sought to demonstrate. In fact, Durkheim's insistence is that we return to a "world," however textual that world is. Texts, discourses, myths, and the entire realm of collective symbols are part of a social world, a world that both underlies *and* is signified by the realm and range of cultural forms and forces. Durkheim's masterful depiction of the power of the collective symbol can also serve to direct social scientific inquiries into the *life of symbols* and, particularly, the grip that collective symbols have over minds and sentiments. His theory also includes the proviso that inquiries be made into the generation of collective symbols in politics, groups, and organizations, and through their collective and public rituals. Since minds are "colonized, we should at least try to examine the colonizing process" (Douglas 1986, p. 97).

Furthermore, to insist, after Lévi-Strauss, that everything "factual" is discursive does not require that one embrace a nihilism or an agnosticism about the moorings of these discourses. As sociologists from Marx to Durkheim to Mannheim have argued, there is an institutional base to "cultural production" (Peterson 1976; 1994). Institutions of all sizes and shapes provide a social basis to thinking and to cognition. And it matters whether the colonizers of minds are churchmen, the "militia," American advertising firms, or all of them at the same time!

While we remember Durkheim's legacy through his notion of the power of nonmaterial "social facts," there was always, in fact, a *materiality* to his vision, one that is compatible with contemporary theories about the "materiality" of thought and culture: in studying gods one studies their images; religion has to do with sacred things; morality and norms correspond to the social facts they address. Yet Durkheim's materiality and Lévi-Strauss's peculiar form of reductionism offer us a rich and compelling sociology, a palpable sense of the "force" and "sacred" character of collective ideas, a vision of *la société* brimming with messages and meanings, with rituals and masks, with irresolute solidarities, and with expressions of the inexpressible. This "structuralist" legacy need not lend itself to partisan concerns. It is an invitation to a "lush sociology" (Lévi-Strauss 1976, p. 7).

For the sociology of knowledge, Lévi-Strauss's most consequential legacy as the "father of structuralism" (Kurzweil 1980) is not to be found in his remorseful vision of civilization's accomplishments in this century, nor does it even lie in the scope of his "cultural relativism," his depiction of the savage mind cast against our own, nor in his lyric depictions of lost peoples. Rather, it is contained in his doctrine of the primacy and autonomy of symbolic systems, particularly the way in which, at his urging, the structuralist project situated itself within the purview of its own "discourse on myths" (Derrida 1970, p. 256). That move, however much it was conceived as integral to the science of structuralism, served—probably in a manner more far-reaching than any empiricism since the eighteenth century—to limit and to alter the idea and the project of human and social science while, simultaneously, unsettling what could be described as the Western mind's capacity to have found a neutral (rational) ground from which it could describe and discover brute reality and brute savages. Lévi-Strauss's peculiar ethnography was an ethnography of *all of us*, in which the minds and myths of "civilized" and "savage" peoples could "communicate" to one another variants of a myth. His structuralist methods opened up new and disturbing forms of self-awareness and self-analysis and served as critical commentaries on ethnographic discourse itself.

4

SELF KNOWLEDGES
The American tradition

I think that a new pole has been constituted by the question, the permanent and
ever-changing question, "What are we today?"

(Michel Foucault)

PRELIMINARY CONSIDERATIONS

The problem of human agency has been considered one of the central problems,
if not the most central, of social analysis. How does one account for human
action or activity without recourse to a primordial "subject" or "individual,"
and within the logic of a thoroughly social idea of the human being as both
creator of its world and created by it. Marx explicitly addressed this dual feature
of human agency, claiming that human beings "make history, but they do not
make it just as they please; they do not make it under circumstances chosen by
themselves, but under circumstances directly encountered, given, and transmitted from the past" (Marx [1869] 1963, p. 15). Others have attempted to
integrate into a single theory this idea that mental life—experience, together
with the forms of knowing and feeling—is not only socially constituted, but is
itself ingredient to action, serving as the source of the continuous change
human societies undergo. In Karl Mannheim's words: the historical subject is
"that kernel of the human personality whose being and dynamism is [sic]
consubstantial with the dominant active forces of history" (Mannheim [1924]
1952, p. 102). Accordingly, while the proper object of social analysis is *society*,
society is understood in a dialectical way, as something continuously made and
inhabited by human beings and, in turn, making them (Berger and Luckmann
1966, p. 456).

While the problem of agency has been addressed by a number of traditions of
social thought, it was the special concern of two relatively distinct traditions
within Western social science, which emerged during the early decades of the
twentieth century in the United States and Germany. In the United States, the
problem of agency was addressed by the *pragmatists*; in Germany, by the framers
of the new discipline called the *sociology of knowledge*. Both traditions sought to
comprehend how individuals think within the particular social context in

which they live; how thinking and consciousness are inherited from particular social and historical contexts; how collective dispositions decisively provide the social objects accessible to human beings. Those working in both traditions also shared an explicit disavowal of traditional philosophies of knowledge and turned to the modern empirical sciences to frame their understanding of the workings of human consciousness and thought.

The German project defined as sociology of knowledge, or *Wissenssoziologie*, was distinguished by its description of thought as a *collective act* in which individuals participate. It is the "impulse to act" in certain groups and with particular styles of thought that "first makes the objects of the world accessible to the acting subject," Mannheim declared in the opening pages of *Ideology and Utopia* (1936). Both he and his contemporary Max Scheler, the original framers of the sociology of knowledge, turned to sociology as a vehicle for approaching the problem of knowledge. In doing so, they explicitly defined and narrowed the subject matter of the broader philosophical problem of the existential roots of thought, focusing on social existence and *knowledge* (see Remmling 1973, pp. 5–6). For Scheler ([1924] 1980, pp. 72–3), who offered the first systematic outline of the discipline, the *forms of mental acts*, through which knowledge is gained, are always co-conditioned by the structure of society. And for this reason, the empirical study of how idea systems are socially based is fundamental to all specialized studies of culture and to metaphysics. For Mannheim, sociology had become a key science whose outlook permeated all the disciplines. In the postliberal age in which he wrote, philosophy no longer adequately reflected the social and intellectual situation: "Today, the internal condition of the social and intellectual situations is reflected most clearly in the diverse forms of sociology" (Mannheim 1936, p. 251).

In the United States, the pragmatist philosopher George Herbert Mead, whose project was far more broadly conceived than that of his German counterparts, set himself the task of elaborating the profoundly social character of mind and consciousness. However, his social theory of mind was similarly grounded in premises compatible with sociology, as the prominent role of his ideas in American sociology has attested. Particularly in his critique of mentalist psychology, Mead demonstrated that subjectivity is socially formed since it presupposes processes of abstraction and interpretation (Mead 1903; [1910] 1964). Investigations of subjectivity, the psychical, and consciousness, he argued, must be made the concern of social science and biological science. This is because psychical phenomena are not "merely subjective"; consciousness is not the property of subjects. Everything conceptualized, everything reflected upon entails language, a social "universe of discourse," and belongs to a common world: "We are beholden to social science to present and analyze the social group with its objects, its interrelations, its selves, as a precondition of our reflective and self-consciousness" (Mead [1910] 1964, pp. 102–3).

C. Wright Mills (1939; 1940), one of the first American sociologists to recognize the affinity of these two projects—American pragmatism and

Wissenssoziologie—argued that the sociology of knowledge be built on insights and terms offered by both traditions: sociology of knowledge offers pragmatism a social and historical field within which human experience and acts have their genesis; pragmatism offers sociology the precise terms and dynamics whereby social factors, in the form of ideas, beliefs, and knowledges, become intrinsic to mind.

However real the differences of the American and German approaches, from our vantage point today, these projects meld with respect to the "pragmatist" qualities of Mannheim's and Scheler's formulations regarding thought and existence: mind was conceived as an *activity*; mental attitudes and knowledge were always linked up with action. Scheler's essay "Probleme einer Soziologie des Wissens," first published in 1924, describes mind as "the sum and substance of the acts of the 'knowing being.'" Throughout the essay, Scheler refers to "mental acts" and to the "history of mind." "Mind itself," he writes, "including its power... really and truly unfolds itself" (Scheler [1924] 1980, p. 434). In its unfolding, there is in every case a change in mind's own constitution. The parallels in Mead's theory of the social genesis of mind are striking: mind and meaning originate in the social act; mind unfolds itself as the social process enters into the experience of individuals (Mead [1922] 1964, p. 247; cf. 1938, p. 372; 1934, pp. 133, 329, 332). Perhaps the work that most closely approaches Scheler's "history of mind" is Mead's *Movements of Thought in the Nineteenth Century* (1936), in which the movements of rationalism and romanticism are seen as stages in the very structures of mind and self in Western history.

According to Kenneth Stikkers (1980, pp. 24–5), despite Scheler's strong criticisms of the American pragmatist tradition, he nonetheless identified as "genius" the pragmatist insight "that knowledge *neither precedes* our experience of things (*ideae ante res*), as in Platonic idealism, *nor follows from* experience and is based upon the correspondence of a proposition with an objective world (*ideae post res*), as claimed by empiricists (e.g., Aristotle)." Moreover, Scheler asserted that American pragmatism provided the first theoretically viable alternative to the idealist and empiricist traditions, locating knowledge within human acts where it becomes functionalized.

The legacy of both traditions is a view of social existence and of mental life as realms of continual change and emergence. Human agency, or selfhood, is a feature of social being and thereby a continual social formation, subject to the diverse sociocultural landscapes in which it is formed. Mead's theory of "emergence" referred to the "relativity" of the individual and its social world, both of which "mutually determine each other" (Mead [1924–5] 1964, p. 278; [1908] 1964, p. 86). "Selves" and "society," "minds" and the social worlds human beings inhabit are continually in the process of adjustment and change relative to one another. Human action at once constitutes and is constituted by a social world. Human cognition is reconstructive. For "reconstruction is essential to the conduct of an intelligent being in the universe.... What is peculiar to intelligence is that it is a change that involves a mutual reorganization, an adjustment in the organism and a reconstruction of the environment" (Mead 1932, pp. 3–4). Any act of knowing always involves change—change in the world that is known and simultaneous change in the knower. Active minds change the world since they give to the world new meanings and new objects. And these new things reshape the people whose lives are touched by them.

In the case of Mannheim, it was historicism that framed the project of *Wissenssoziologie* and, indeed, provided the principles for grasping the meaning of modernity as a condition of continual change. Historicism was not only an intellectual project or program, it was the intellectual force of the modern age that organized, "like an invisible hand," both the work of the cultural sciences and everyday thinking as well (Mannheim [1924] 1952, p. 84). Historicism sees every aspect of social and personal reality as in a state of continual change and flux. Our worlds and ourselves, Mannheim wrote, are grasped as

potentialities, constantly in flux, moving from some point in time to another; already on the level of everyday reflection, we seek to determine the position of our present within such a temporal framework, to tell by the cosmic clock of history what the time is. Our view of life has already become thoroughly sociological and sociology is just one of those spheres which, increasingly dominated by the principle of historicism, reflect most faithfully our new orientation in life.

As if speaking of today instead of the year 1924, Mannheim wrote that it is impossible to engage in life or even to grasp the meaning of our own lives "without treating all those realities which we have to deal with as having evolved and as developing" ([1924] 1952, p. 84). As a world view, historicism followed upon the dissolution of the medieval picture of the world and upon the self-destroying idea, born of Enlightenment, of a supratemporal Reason (p. 85). As a world view, historicism functioned as that principle pervading "every phase of our world experience" (p. 126), serving as "the very basis on which we construct our observations of the socio-cultural reality" (p. 85).

THE SELF AS AGENT AND SOCIAL OBJECT

The relative and changing character of mind and society was a working presupposition of both Mead's pragmatist social psychology and Mannheim's sociology of knowledge. However, it is to Mead that the social sciences are indebted for providing a fully developed theory of human agency that could account for the relativity of the individual and its social world—what Berger and Luckmann (1966) termed the "dialectic of objective and subjective reality." That theory introduced the term "the self" or the social self, by which Mead meant the conscious self-reflective ego or agent through which human experience is organized and interpreted and with which it encounters and deals with its world. Mead argued that the very capacity for self-conscious agency originates in social relations and exchanges, since these provide the dialogical and dramatic qualities that characterize human conscious life and its reflexive capacity.

The self's essential characteristic is reflexiveness: *the self is an object to itself*, capable of entering its own experience, at first indirectly, by becoming an object to itself. This occurs in childhood as one gradually becomes conscious of the attitudes and roles of others within a social environment in which both self and other are implicated. Considered this way, self-consciousness is organized from the outside in, proceeding from object-consciousness to a consciousness of self that is, in its earliest childhood experiences, principally formed out of a consciousness of others' actions and perspectives directed our way, that is, *toward the self as a singular object*. In other words, the self first appears as a third person, principally in the speech, but also the gestures and attitudes of others; the self appears as an *object* brought into consciousness with other objects and other selves. In Mead's terms, *the self is a social object, inseparable from the social relations and the forms of speech within which it is communicated.* As with all social objects, its form is found in the experiences of other selves, experiences that are inseparable from a common linguistic medium (Mead 1934, p. 142). Language—understood in its larger context of social cooperation, which takes place through the mutual exchange and interpretation of signs and gestures—*is* the activity in which selves are constituted. For it provides the kinds of activity in which individuals can become objects to themselves.

The importance of this theory, sketched out only briefly here, is that it provides an account of how social reality, an objective action complex at first comprised of the immediate social and linguistic community of the child, enters into the developing experience of that child, and how the roles and attitudes of the others with whom the child interacts serve to awaken in the child a sense of itself as the object of others' acts. Accordingly, the human being's first knowledge of itself originates in a consciousness of "me," an object which it sweeps into its own field of experience (Mead 1934, p. 138). The self's "me" exists first as an object among other objects and within the same field of experience. Self-consciousness is a further development and refinement of this social process and occurs when one *becomes aware of one's own responses* and, thereby, *self-conscious*—aware of oneself as an object toward which the child can now respond as an "I." Responses to ourselves can be seen when "we are sometimes afraid of our own anger," when we "work on our own sentiment . . . are aware of our daydreams . . . and find ourselves replying to our response—we fear, admire, sympathize with ourselves" (Mead [1914] 1982, p. 53). These responses are communicated to ourselves and are instances of a self-consciousness that presupposes *self-objectification*, a consciousness of our own objectivity, or a consciousness of our own *otherness* in a world of others (Crapanzano 1992, p. 79).

Responses to the self (actually, the *awareness* of these responses) become the materials for a fully developed selfhood, continuously enriched and elaborated in the form of inner dialogues that recapitulate the dialogical life we share with others. Mead described the two voices of these self-exchanges as the "I," the active voice of the individual, and the "me," the self-as-object. Each of these is an element in the self's developing self-concept and self-consciousness. The self "becomes an object to himself, through the very fact that he hears himself talk, and replies" (Mead [1913] 1964, p. 146). In the adult, the reply is typically silent—he imagines the response that his "vocal gesture" calls out in another. With regard to the child, however, Mead's statement takes on literal meaning. The child carries on a conversation with himself, and the responses of others that he produces in play are the building blocks of self-consciousness. For in the act of becoming another, children are able to take up a conversation with themselves (Mead 1934, pp. 150–1).

The articulation of a self occurs in and through this dialogue of the "I" and the "me" phases of the self, revealing how both the form of self-conscious life and its particular linguistic and cultural content (the words, idioms, and ethos out of which selfhood is formed) are ineluctably social and cultural, involving the self's recognition of its various capacities to respond to the social meanings of the objects it experiences. As Hans Joas (1985, p. 110) contends,

> In Mead's opinion there is a continuous development, extending from the immediately dialogical structure of the self-consciousness of the child, who speaks to itself in the words of its parents, to the most abstract processes of thought. In the course of this development, the direct connection to particular persons of the individual parts of the internal process of communication ... becomes weaker; but the mechanism is unchanged and remains a social one.

Joas then cites Mead's 1913 article "The Social Self," in which this argument is elaborated and emphasized (see Mead [1913] 1964, pp. 146–7):

> Until this process has been developed into the abstract process of thought, self-consciousness remains dramatic, and the self which is a fusion of the remembered actor and this accompanying chorus is somewhat loosely organized and very clearly social. Later the inner state changes into the forum and workshop of thought. The features and intonations of the dramatis personae fade out and the emphasis falls upon the meaning of the inner speech, the imagery becomes merely the barely necessary cues. But the mechanism remains social, and at any moment the process may become personal.

Selfhood refers to the capacity not only to take ourselves as objects but also to *objectify* our experiences and to act in relation to them—to signify or to *say* something or to make something of these experiences while, at the same time, referring them to ourselves and to others. This self-reflexive capacity *is* what a self is; it "provides the core and the primary structure of the self" (Mead 1934,

p. 173). Whether the *emotions* we feel, the *other* with whom we are immediately engaged, or an *idea* we have of our tomorrow, each of these *social objects* is the "stuff" of human action and signification. Social objects not only serve to fill up the "rooms" human beings occupy, although they certainly serve that purpose too; social objects of all shapes and sizes are there to converse with and about—we hold them out to others to be admired, stand on them to make speeches, toss them about in anger (all of this, both literally and figuratively). For social objects not only include the many and varied "things" that surround us and that we speak about but also serve as signs for us *to speak with*: clothing and other objects of adornment, beer cans, motherhood, motorcycles, laughter and other gestures involving the body, and even the emotions can serve as signifying gestures. However different each of these things are, their likeness derives from the use human beings can make of them, becoming at any moment *signifying objects* for the communication of something to ourselves and to others.

Herbert Blumer described social life as the habitat of beings who "make indications" to themselves about the multitude of objects surrounding them—the ticking of a clock, the smell of cologne, the color of someone's stocking, the tilt of a hat, or the rush of embarrassment that suddenly overtakes one. "The conscious life of the human being . . . is a continual flow of self-indications—notations of the things with which he deals and takes into account"(Blumer 1969, p. 80). Social objects—anything that a human being indicates to itself—have this twofold capacity described above: first, as objects, they are referred to and acted toward; second, *as signs in their own right*, social objects can be used to signify something to others, to "make statements," to be used as props in the enactment of a role, as signs of impending disaster. All social objects have this dual capacity to serve as objects of social action and as signs that enable action to proceed. Emotions, for example, not only serve as objects of elaborate social ritual and practice but also as signs of who and what we are, as things we handle in our presentation of self. Freud ([1923] 1960) and, more recently, Hochschild (1983) have written extensively about this signal function of emotions.

In his essay "The Meaning of Suffering," Max Scheler (1992, p. 83) also describes emotional experiences as a differentiated system of signs with which the self engages. There are, he argues, "*styles* of feeling and of willing" that presuppose an interpreting agent or self, objectifying its emotional experience and subjecting it to a system of meaning such as a "doctrine of suffering." Such doctrines are today described under the rubric of "discourses," an organization of written and spoken forms, an area of language-use identified by particular historical groups and institutions. Historically these "doctrines," forming parts of discourses (religious, psychiatric, medical, etc.), have offered to human beings ways of encountering suffering (Scheler 1992, p. 97): "suffering has been objectified, resigned to, tolerated, escaped from, dulled to the point of apathy, heroically struggled against, justified as deserved punishment, and denied." Accordingly, "we can 'give ourselves up' to suffering, 'tolerate' it, or simply 'suffer'; we can even 'enjoy' suffering (algophilia). These phrases signify *styles* of feeling and of willing based on feeling, which are clearly not determined by the mere state of feeling" (p. 83). Furthermore, they imply a social actor drawing on whatever repertory exists at her disposal to make something out of her experiences to validate the things she knows and believes about herself and the social worlds she encounters with others.

OBJECTS AND OTHERS IN THE GENESIS OF SELF

As the preceding discussion has shown, human agency, far from an innate condition, involves a developing awareness of objects against and through which human self-awareness is formed. C. H. Cooley's formulation ([1909] 1983, p. 5) that "self and society are twin born" was intended to capture this point precisely. Early self-consciousness, he argued, is characterized by a definite, although limited, ability to arouse in oneself the responses of others, bestowing on them "objectivity." This process allows for one's own "objectivity" to develop—what Crapanzano (1992, p. 79) identifies as "one's own otherness" in a world of others.

How these "objects," so critical to human and social development, are construed varies across the modern academic disciplines. Yet despite the differences, there are some clear family resemblances in the functions objects serve in the cognitive development of selfhood. For example, in three fields— the psychology of perception, phenomenology, and psychoanalysis—the physical resistance objects offer to the developing capacities of human beings are discussed: objects provide the conditions that enable human beings to become conscious of their difference as separate entities and agencies in their relation to the objects they confront and with which they "converse." In this sense, the real world of objects, existing independently of the human child, can be said to *emerge*, an argument also found among the pragmatists (e.g., Mead 1938, Part II). Resistance in contact experience confirms the reality of objects, while simultaneously bestowing on human beings a sense of their own reality over and against these things (e.g., Schachtel 1959; Schutz 1971, pp. 306ff.; Bowlby 1969).

In social science and social psychology, we find arguments bearing a remarkable resemblance to these (e.g., in psychology and phenomenology), concerning the foundational role of both personal and physical objects in the social origins of selfhood and the formation and maintenance of personal and social identity. In the case of social science, however, emphasis is placed on the importance of "the group" and of sociocultural goods or "material culture" (e.g., Douglas and Isherwood 1978). Highlighting some of these arguments, personal and physical objects are viewed on the same logical level with the self, providing points of reference for both self-definition and continuity, as well as the materials for social processes of exchange and bargaining. Objects also form the basis for status claims and for social conflict or envy. For a number of sociologists who have written classic works in sociology, such as Thorstein Veblen ([1899] 1967), Georg Simmel ([1908] 1950), and William Graham Sumner ([1906] 1940), physical objects for consumption or for adornment enlarge or intensify the personality, serve as vehicles in the constitution of sentiments and social attitudes, as ever-present reminders of social identities, making them materially present while also serving as emblems of self, status, and group membership. More neutrally, objects serve as "marks" (Schutz 1971, pp. 308–9), as reminders or devices for action, thus providing human beings with the vital means to find or to maintain their bearings in everyday life. Objects provide a persistent and endless source of personal and group consistency and continuity, or they can be used to mark off the boundaries of a me-world where the self finds itself "at home," or in spaces and places where one resides as a member of a tribe, clan, nation, or family (e.g., Csikszentmihalyi and Rochberg-Halton 1981; Dittmar 1992).

But human groups also serve functions that parallel those of physical things: throughout history, women and wives, children, slaves and servants have served as valuable possessions and emblems of social standing. Or, individuals and groups, much like physical things, serve as the foundation from which human beings derive a sense of sameness or difference. For a social identity is built up *in relation to* others with whom we feel alike and those whose otherness or difference is responsible for the "who" or the "what" we are—our social identity.

Throughout his extensive writings on the social self, Mead described a *social and cooperative relationship* between human beings and their personal and physical environments. His writings addressed the vital function objects serve in both human perception and conception: objects are foundational to self-conscious selfhood, providing the conditions for a consciousness of *difference* as a separate entity and agency. Objects simultaneously provide selves with a knowledge of *commonality*, a sense of sameness or a common character that selves share with other objects. Mead described this process as one of *identification* (1932, pp. 121–2; 1934, pp. 168–73; 1938, pp. 163–4, 327–31, 426–32): identification of the individual with an object is the condition for self-reflexiveness. Even on the level of contact with material things, identification is the means by which the individual moves from a knowledge of the "insides" of things to the "inside" of one's bodily self—a movement from object to subject, from other to me. The active physical resistance of the things that one encounters provides a "common character" to things and to ourselves, for resistance is experienced as coming from the "insides" of things human beings encounter (Mead 1938, pp. 212–13).

But without Mead's emphasis on the semiotic and self-referential features of object relations (Cohen 1989; 1993), the self–object relation remains a relatively static and mechanistic model and surely not a cultural one. Mead's own particular focus on the social and interactional basis of self-reflexiveness and on the importance of the "cooperative" relationship human beings have with physical things—his idea of the self as both agent and object of signification—opens the way for a theory of *identity* that is not only *social*, involving the interaction of social actors whose acts reverberate in and throughout a vast network of social structures, but a *cultural* one as well. For the communication of meaning is its paramount feature, and the processes of becoming aware of oneself involve "language gestures" at every step of the way.

Mead's "genesis of the self" is described as a process requiring a consciousness of the Other. Only by placing oneself within the shared "attitude" of the Other does self-conscious selfhood fully emerge, finding one's own experiences in the response of the Other and articulated in the shared terms of the group. The philosopher David Miller (1973, p. 101) summarizes these ideas this way:

> The distinction between subjective and objective cannot arise until awareness arises, and awareness involves taking the role of the other, an other which is certainly there and not in the mind. One can become aware of himself only by having in his own experience both the stimulus phase and the response phase of the social act, and such awareness requires language gestures evoking responses that are shareable by another participant.

REVISITING THE CLASSICAL THEMES OF IDENTITY AND COMMUNITY

In modern societies, as in their social and psychological sciences, the theme of *identity* has been paramount, precisely because the place of the self in the shifting world of modernity has been rendered problematic. A long-standing modern motif is the apparent fragmentation of personal identity due to the rise of industrial culture and its weakening of the great stabilizing and integrating forces of human existence (religion, labor, and language), and their replacement by the vast, complex, and artificial structures of technical civilization.

The themes of *identity* and *community* together capture the modernist problem of the individual's standing within a social order—"community" designating the location in space (homogeneous, unified, participating in shared values) from which individuals derive both personal meaning and the cultural means for entering into a "society" with others. From classical to contemporary social thought, the nature of modern communities has been examined through a series of binary oppositions: *Gemeinschaft* and *Gesellschaft*, mechanical and organic, folk and urban, status and contract, traditional and modern, primary and secondary groups—oppositions designating the gradual replacement of traditional, stable, relatively homogeneous life-worlds with the changing, complex, and unstabilizing character of industrial societies.

Using a sociology-of-knowledge approach to these themes (that is also thoroughly historical), we can grasp the originality of these collective experiences throughout the modern era and use it to understand the ways that

73

these experiences have recently changed—not fundamentally as the postmodernists claim, but in ways that are, in fact, continuous with modernism. In addressing these changes, we will turn to questions of what revisionist work needs to be done so that the problem of identity, as our discipline understands it and studies it, is responsive to some of the national and global developments that most affect issues of identity and community today, and to the emergence of new processes of identity since mid-century. For example, some contemporary social theorists have argued that modernity in this half century is distinguished by an increasing interconnection between the globalizing influences of societies and the personal and highly reflexive dispositions of social actors (Giddens 1991). Others, such as Aronowitz (1992), emphasize the fact that people share multiple social identities, irreducible to class and local communities.

Modernism contains within it a thoroughly social and historical idea of the human being—its experience, mental life, and its particular social identity as subject to change. For human agency or selfhood is a feature of social being, and thereby a continual social formation, subject to the diverse sociocultural landscapes in which it is formed. But modernism also means that human subjectivity (experience, together with the forms of knowing and feeling) is itself ingredient to action, serving as the source of the continual change human societies undergo. Modernism brings with it a particular consciousness about self and society, one that not only demands social and political changes and renewals, but also renewals that only men and women themselves can bring about. Asserting this modernist standard, Marshall Berman claims, "Modern men and women must become the subjects as well as the objects of modernization; they must learn to change the world that is changing them, and to make it their own" (1992, p. 33).

Accordingly, the recent instances of the democratization of the world order since 1989 can be read as instances of the worldwide dissemination of modernist culture in the realm of the political—as "modernism in the streets" (Berman 1992, p. 33). Yet modernism is also at work in the growing recognition by more groups and classes that choice extends into the realm of personal identity—that the self is "made" reflexively. The social psychologist Kenneth Gergen (1991) calls this "consciousness of construction," affecting relationships and identity. Yet as early as 1951, in his now classic article "Identification as the Basis for a Theory of Motivation," Nelson Foote wrote of people's commitments to particular identities arising through a process whereby conceptions of self are acquired, confirmed, revised, and elaborated by others and oneself—a description that highlights the highly reflexive character of modern consciousness and activity, about which Anthony Giddens writes. Even our futures, Giddens has argued, do not just consist of the expectations of events to come. Rather, "futures" are "organized reflexively in the present in terms of the chronic flow of knowledge into the environments about which such knowledge was developed." In this context, *people's personal*

74

lives and identities are perceived as processes of active intervention, choice, and transformation (Giddens 1991, p. 29).

There is what could be called a *democratic idiom* at work in the domain of selfhood—one that infuses contemporary ideas and standards of *what a self is*—just as there is a democratic idiom that has profoundly directed the course of modern politics, its markets, and the institutions and relations of the modern social order. This idiom or characteristic style that the self has assumed simultaneously serves to foster and to legitimate *the project of selfhood*. For it contains the idea that whatever I understand myself to be, I can and should articulate that selfhood, express its opinions, value its judgments, and demand that others do so. Accordingly, I expect that my future, and those of other selves, is something I make happen, not something undergone as much as realized and achieved through my own efforts, choices, and decisions.

Modernism then is not a term only attached to culture and to social structure, as if these reside outside of selves, it is also a drama played out on the level of our "psychologies" and in the standards and expectations we impose on ourselves and others about such matters as bodily and verbal gesture or expression of feeling, and so forth. Perhaps most of all, modernism refers to the recognition (if we may call it that without undermining our argument) that there are struggles and battles of *selfhood* to be waged and won (or lost, as the case may be); that the self is a project, or, to use an effective if trite metaphor, the self is a drama played out over time and in space, a drama beginning at birth and ending only with death. It is not that selfhood and the life of emotions and sentiments did not exist at all before. Rather, it is that so very "much is made of them"—a theme traced in Charles Taylor's wide-ranging study of the sources of modern selfhood (1989, p. 292).

The vast literature on the modern self's interior landscape—from Freud, Durkheim, and Tocqueville to contemporary works in social psychology—portrays modern identity as multiple, personal, and highly reflexive; distant and detached rather than embedded in social roles and traditions; other-directed (Riesman *et al.* 1950) or interpersonally competent in the skills of reading cues from others, yet dependent on them for recognition. Anxiety and crises of growth and change have become assumed traits that changing selves must meet and undergo; feelings and emotions, however fleeting and unsubstantial, have come to serve as among the principal experiences of self-validation, as the moorings from which to claim an identity and to build a self-conception; both the self and the body are viewed as *projects*, significant objects of attention and action in contrast to the view of them as natural objects; one's identity is "built up," yet also "discovered," and one's "emotional life" a vehicle for rendering one's life and one's identity meaningful. A "new subjectivism" (Gehlen [1949] 1980), its emphasis on inner elaboration and "psychologization," represents the modern self's attempt to control the flood of stimuli that often overtaxes our ability to respond, turning the subject inward where experiences are monitored in states of heightened awareness and reflection. It is within this situation that psychology and psychoanalysis have acquired the standing of a world view, defending the "private" person against the demands of culture, elaborating further its sense of separateness from the world.

We can, then, speak broadly of a modern Western identity, recognizing its limits with respect to differences of class, race, gender, historical period, and so forth, claiming that particular historical societies engender particular experiences of selfhood and even different degrees of articulation of subjectivity and objectivity (see Crapanzano 1992, pp. 73ff.). Surely this was the idea behind Weber's ([1904–5] 1958, p. 154) notion of the Puritan's "inner worldly asceticism." ("Christian asceticism . . . strode into the market-place of life . . . undertook to penetrate just that daily routine of life with its methodicalness, to fashion it into a life in the world. . . . ") This idea of the distinct form of modern selfhood was what Tocqueville described as "democratic individualism" and was the basis of perhaps the earliest theory of the origin of Western individuality by Burckhardt ([1890] 1954), who located it in the changing political circumstances in Italy during the Renaissance.

Before modernity, Burckhardt argued, it was as if human consciousness lay hidden under a veil—a "veil woven of faith, illusion, and childish prepossession." When this veil "melted into air," the objective world and all the things of this world became possible. "The subjective side at the same time asserted itself with corresponding emphasis: [the human being] became a spiritual individual, and recognized itself as one" ([1890] 1954, p. 100).

According to these observations, crosscultural and historical differences of peoples are expressed in the different concepts of self, socially and politically engendered and symbolically mediated. But *difference* can also be discovered in the experiences of peoples within the same society as, for instance, when marginalized peoples must struggle against the conceptions of themselves of their dominant Others. Robert Park described this eloquently through his account of the social *marginality* of immigrant Jews and Negroes in America (1950, pp. 284–300, 345–56, 372–6). W. E. B. Du Bois ([1903] 1989, p. 5) captured it in his account of the Negro American's "double-consciousness" and "double-selfhood"—this "peculiar sensation . . . of always looking at one's self through the eyes of others, of measuring one's soul by the tape of a world that looks on in amused contempt and pity." Dorothy Smith, in her feminist sociology (1987), describes that "line of fault" from which she began to recognize that the only means of expression and knowledge available to women were made and controlled by men—knowledges in which she and all other women were the Other.

However painfully wrought in the lives of marginalized groups and persons, the discovery of self always, in principle, involves the discovery of *the Other*—a consciousness of "me," an object of others' perspectives and acts—which it sweeps into its own field of experience. Self-consciousness is a further development and refinement of this process, involving an awareness of one's own responses to these experiences. Each of these—a me-ness derived socially and a self-conscious response to this derivative self—is expressed in Du Bois's "double-consciousness," a gift of "second-sightedness," a "two-ness" in his being: an American, an African-American—"two-souls, two thoughts, two unreconciled strivings. . . ." Self-consciousness, then, entails self-objectifica-tion—a consciousness of our own objectivity, or a consciousness of our own otherness in a world of others (Crapanzano 1992, p. 79). Each of these accounts contains the baffling assertion that individuality is collectively based; that the discovery of self, emerging self-consciousness, and finally, a self-identity are inextricably linked to the discovery of an Other—even an alien or hostile Other, the recognition in some "objective" way of one's own otherness in the face of the Other—in the face of an entity that is not-me.[1]

To summarize several contemporary positions that converge in a number of important ways, "identity" is a social process involving a *dialectics of sameness and difference*, a process of forming and sustaining a self-concept and its attendant self-feelings as they become objectified in and through dialogues with a collective or "generalized" Other (Mead 1934, p. 152). A "social identity" is the self signified *as something* or *as someone*, a signification addressed both *to oneself and to others* with whom one converses and where culture, in the form of language—concepts and discourses—operates at every phase of this dialogue.

> Social identification is a process in which people come to feel that some other human beings are much "the same" as they are and still others are more "unlike" them . . . [occurring] as part of the dialectics of inclusion and exclusion from which groups emerge in a dynamics of competition.
>
> (de Swaan 1992, p. 1)

"The self," Perinbanayagam claims, "is an assemblage of signs, a more or less coherent text that a mind claims as its own and identifies as a presence in a world of others." Self-identification is a process of activating a presence in a world of objects and others and involves *identification with* and *disidentification from* (1991, pp. 12–13). Self-identity is a semiotic formation where difference and similarity are established visually through bodily signs, such as clothing (Davis 1992), actively in and through social practices, and, especially, discursively—in speaking (Perinbanayagam 1991). For in conversing with others we are constructing ourselves: "Dialogues," the anthropologist Crapan-zano claims, "are always dramas of self-constitution" (1992, p. 130)—whether the dialogues of analyst and analysand of which this author writes, or the "dialogues" we conduct with others near and far; those we know closely or those remote others who make up our "society." We converse with our contempor-aries who are known to us in varying degrees of intimacy and familiarity, or of strangeness and anonymity (Schutz 1971, p. 16). We converse with our predecessors and successors (Schutz 1971, pp. 15–16), the meaning and reality of whose lives may be of even greater personal value to us than those of neighbor and kin.

"I know more of the lives of Martin Luther, Karl Marx, and Thomas Jefferson than I do of either of my own grandfathers," Craig Calhoun writes, in a theoretical essay on the complex nature of contemporary human relations and communities (1991, p. 114). He describes how people today think of themselves as members of large collectivities of others with whom there are almost no direct interpersonal relations: nations, races, and genders, but also the National Rifle Association, the National Organization for Women, the Boy Scouts of America, and so forth. These are "imagined" but no less real communities of others with whom we identify: other Americans, Brits, Bosnians, gays, black sisters, pro-lifers—others, for example, whom one "imagines" as having a shared past, a destiny, a common victimhood, a set of passions, dispositions, or interests. In such a process, described by Abram de Swaan (1992) as a "dialectics of inclusion and exclusion," group identification or likeness can be as vital to one's selfhood as the sense of being unlike and set in opposition to the Other. In many instances, such "imagined communities" (so called by Benedict Anderson in his book of the same name) adopt the ancient and traditional ideas of tribe and family to form lineages of common ancestry or imagine themselves as part of a brotherhood or sisterhood.

Anderson's book (1991) is a study of the origins and global spread of nationalism, from the Americas to popular movements in Europe. Nationalism was part of the history of Western imperialism but was also adopted by the anti-imperialist resistances in Asia and Africa. Anderson explores the many processes that created these national communities. Vitally important was the use of printing—newspapers and books. "Print capitalism" made it possible for peoples to think about themselves in new ways, as existing simultaneously across vast spaces, but also as linked with others like ourselves back into a past and forwards into a future.

→ A nation is

> an imagined political community... *imagined* because the members of even the smallest nation will never know most of their fellow-members, meet them, or even hear of them, yet in the minds of each lives the image of their communion.... [A]ll communities larger than primordial villages of face-to-face contact (and perhaps even these) are imagined. Communities are to be distinguished, not by their falsity/genuineness, but by the style in which they are imagined,

whether as networks of kin living and dead, or in the style of modern economic classes, which, if we go back before the eighteenth century, were *unimaginable* (Anderson 1991, p. 6).

Such was E. P. Thompson's claim in his path-breaking book *The Making of the English Working Class*. Its central idea is that of *modern identity*, arguing that "In the years between 1780 and 1832 most English working people came to feel

78

an identity of interests as between themselves, and as against their rulers and employers" (1963, pp. 11–12). Historically, collective identities have been formed out of opposition and resistance (Burke 1992), through which the "idea of the people," as nation and as working class, spread (p. 294). Today these "imagined communities" have become commonplace, but also far more varied.

Imagined communities/imagined selves

In the preceding pages, we have moved quickly from a summary of some formal tenets (albeit culturally constructed ones) in social science and social psychology regarding the social genesis of self and self-identity, to historically specific instances regarding identity and community in the modern period. In doing so, I have introduced what some today regard as a series of new social phenomena—the growth of "imagined communities" and indirect relationships—that invites revisionist formulations about identities, how they are formed and sustained, culturally and politically. Despite the fact that sociology's modern classics identified (and also disseminated) the problem of the individual and society—of identity and community—I agree with the formulation offered by Calhoun (in his 1991 article on this topic), that these aspects of modernity remain "sociologically undertheorized" (p. 95): including the effects of such contemporary phenomena as the divide between public and private sectors in contemporary life; including the perceived split between the realm of public life with its vast, complex systems and that of private everyday life; and also with respect to the increasingly typical phenomenon of indirect relationships that prevail over those of local and direct face-to-face relations— what M. W. Webber has termed the rise of "communities without propinquity" (cited in Calhoun 1991, p. 101). Direct relations undoubtedly remain important and effective today, but they are circumscribed; their meanings are changed by the effects of indirect relations—such as those of organizations, associations, political and cultural movements, youth cultures—imagined communities that compete with family, friend, and neighbor for our loyalty, affection, and commitment.

Calhoun points to the importance of the commonalities linking the rise of highly indirect relations mediated by technology and complex organizations with other more commonplace phenomena: particularly objects and images of identification transmitted through mass media and television, such as characters in soap operas, celebrities and entertainers, athletes and politicians (the latter two sharing in the Showbiz aura of the former). Each of these social figures is typically perceived today as if she or he exists for the audiences in real and familiar ways, belying a kind of *identity* established between mass media figures and their viewers or, say, between the personalities and lives of people whose biographies we read and to whom we grow "personally" attached. This may account for today's extensive and diverse public taste for biographies and for TV and print tabloids that examine celebrities' lives. For supermarket tabloids that report about the lives and antics of celebrities signify far more than simply the public's taste for sex, scandal, and scoops about the "rich and famous." They reveal a sustained interest in and identification with the ongoing lives of these familiar strangers: "familiar strangers" identifies what indirect relationships are—we feel close to them, a certain attachment, or even a sense of intimacy with them. Yet, they are, in fact, unknown and unknowable to us. (See, for example, Schickel's 1986 study of the public's knowledge of celebrities as an imaginary intimacy fostered by the media and Braudy's 1986 comprehensive study of the culture of fame.)

What these examples signify is a collective disposition for new forms of relationships that simulate traditional and communal direct relations of neighbors, relatives, and friends. The capacity of broadcast media to "simulate directness of relationship" (Calhoun 1991, p. 110) is obviously an important feature of this phenomenon, as is its capacity to offer for popular consumption "categorical identities" or social types—men and women, people growing older, working-class and rich, African-Americans, cops and criminals, and so forth—for "first-hand" observation and knowledge of them. Some of them provide effective images for building identities, others confirm a sense of difference and exclusion. Sports events and political conventions provide similar arenas for identities to be dramatized and played out—occasions for the enactment of "identity politics," for revelling in the images and antics, the victories and defeats of those with whom we feel "the same" and those whom we wish to exclude. Broadcast media, seen perhaps best in its proliferation of "talk shows" for the ordinary person to "speak their mind," provides yet another occasion for us to play out and to work through the confusing and changing spectacles taking place in the United States today.

As the shape of our communities alter in time and in space, people continue to seek out and to discover themselves in and through these groups, these others from which they derive both commonality and difference. That is perhaps why imagined communities, such as nations, as well as those of race and gender, "arouse such deep attachments" (Parker *et al.* 1992, p. 4): the nation and others of my race and sex represent to me "a deep, horizontal comradeship," a brotherhood or sisterhood reaching backwards in time and stretching out into the future, providing a continuity we seek in our world and in ourselves. Particularly if we are fated to live today with an unprecedented consciousness of our own construction as selves (affecting our relationships and our identities) on another level of our consciousness, we seek out eternal structures and verities.

On a far less speculative note, our identities and communities are no longer as circumscribed in time and space as those of the modernists who wrote the classic texts of our discipline. The idea of community and culture that once contained the "expectation of roots, of a stable, territorialized existence" (Clifford 1988, p. 338) no longer addresses the worlds of many of us today. We respond to different metaphors, such as migration, dispersion, and travel.

Those social scientists who have used these terms, principally anthropologists, have been sensitized to the global developments that have rendered "community" and "identity" and "culture" far more complex and multilayered than they had been for their predecessors. This is undoubtedly because anthropologists are in the business of providing ethnographies of foreign "non-Western" peoples (designations that today sound dated and even prejudicial). Anthropologists were some of the first to document the diffusion of modernism worldwide, and the presence of world cultures and peoples in our midst. "This century," Clifford writes in *The Predicament of Culture*,

> has seen a drastic expansion of mobility, including tourism, migrant labor, immigration, urban sprawl. More and more people "dwell" with the help of mass transit, automobiles, airplanes.... The "exotic" is uncannily close ... there seem no distant places left on the planet where the presence of "modern" products, media, and power cannot be felt. An older topography and experience of travel is exploded.... Difference is encountered in the adjoining neighborhood, the familiar turns up at the ends of the earth.
>
> (1988, pp. 13–14)

"WHAT ARE WE TODAY?"

Whether in its theories of "community" or in its social theories of "self," social science has not taken its own *social* premises to their conclusion. Nor has our thinking been adequately historical or cultural in our investigations into self and subjectivity. Our categories ("society" and "social structure") have been remarkably devoid of cultural forms and forces—language, image, symbol, meaning. Is it any wonder that we did not develop a strong sense of the human capacity to adorn ourselves (and to be adorned...) in the glitter of cultural forms, and to understand how rich and varied these forms are when wrapped and draped about human figures we call "selves?" Additionally, and as many have pointed out, in places like the United States the powerful prejudice that we are "individuals" has undermined any effective sense that culture really matters as far as real people are concerned (Riesman 1954; Dumont 1986; Heller *et al.* 1986). And the image of "individuals" is of a faceless crowd (of individuals?) or of beings unadorned, stripped down to their "inalienable rights" and freedoms.

But from where we stand today, "history" and "culture" are defining us, not only in the academic theories we spin but in the consciousness of everyday life, where the notion has been gaining ground that "culture" *is* a fact and a force making us different from one another, sometimes in profound and inescapable ways. Alongside this *consciousness of culture* is another consciousness that exists in tension with the first: a *"consciousness of construction"* (Gergen 1991, pp. 146ff.), a sense that there are "selves" and "identities" to conquer and to claim as our own.

While these two marks of our mentality may appear to be in conflict—that language and culture profoundly shape us, and that selfhood is something variable and something that *we* can fashion—they effectively serve to create the sense that selves today are profoundly variable beings, in thrall to mundane forces (groups, society, culture), while simultaneously lacking foundations either in the order of being (ontology) or in nature. This inescapable "recognition" fosters in us a sense of our "construction": the self and the body have become "sites of interaction," worked on by the techniques and the practitioners of high modernity. Today, neither the body nor one's identity is viewed as a natural object; each is increasingly subject to discursive practices and reflexive action, the kinds provided by self-help texts and techniques, therapies, exercise machinery and manuals, sex changes, plastic surgery for breasts and for noses (*inter alia*), organ transplants. "The body itself," Giddens writes, "as mobilised in praxis . . . becomes more immediately relevant to the identity the individual promotes" (1991, p. 218) or to an identity promoted by a society. The body is that last domain of privacy and secrecy, that site of emancipatory acts and politics, that Western "code" of pleasure (Foucault 1980b, p. 191).

The self and the body have, in fact, become cultural formations, in ways that they were not before. By asserting this, I am claiming that as cultural objects they are subjected to more extensive and diverse cultural practices and operations than the selves and bodies of our forebears. I am also asserting that the quality of people's self-reflexive actions has effectively rendered both selves and bodies as *sites* on which their actions and desires can be played out and played with: the domain of "nature" (self, body) has been rendered "culture." The context for this event is contemporary life—the landscape of high modernity, with reflexive features built into virtually all of its aspects (Giddens 1991). Reflexivity especially distinguishes our forms of selfhood and the unfolding and seemingly uncharted and ungrounded domain of identity.

"Self-fashioning," as Greenblatt calls it, is not an invention of modernity; there were selves and "a sense that they could be fashioned" (1980, p. 1) before this epoch. But what *was* born in the early modern era of the sixteenth century was both an "increased self-consciousness about the fashioning of human identity as a manipulable, artful process" and a new-found sense of autonomy: "the power to impose a shape upon oneself is an aspect of the more general power to control identity—that of others at least as often as one's own" (Greenblatt 1980, p. 1; cf. Elias 1978, p. 79).

Within modernity and late modernity, the assertion of an autonomous or an individual self lives on as our consciousness of the power of culture intensifies. Greenblatt makes a similar observation when he remarks, at the close of his treatise on "self-fashioning," that he

> perceived that fashioning oneself and being fashioned by cultural institutions—family, religion, state—were inseparately intertwined . . . .

Whenever I focused sharply upon a moment of apparently autonomous self-fashioning, I found not an epiphany of identity freely chosen but a cultural artifact.

(1980, p. 256)

In Foucault's question "What are we today?" we find a similar tension. For the question itself contains within it the recognition of the "made up" self, yet—especially in his later writings—an enlivened sense that our ability to ask the question at all matters a great deal. The question and the questioner signify the *attitude of modernity*:

a mode of relating to contemporary reality; a voluntary choice made by certain people; in the end, a way of thinking and feeling; a way, too, of acting and behaving that at one and the same time marks a relation of belonging and presents itself as a task . . . . And consequently, rather than seeking to distinguish the "modern era" from the "premodern" or "postmodern," I think it would be more useful to try to find out how the attitude of modernity, ever since its formation, has found itself struggling with attitudes of "countermodernity."

(Foucault 1984, p. 39)

"What are we today?" The question, as posed by Foucault, meant what is that "field of the historical reflection on ourselves?" (1988, p. 4). The question was that of modern philosophers—Kant, Nietzsche, Husserl, Heidegger, and others. But the question referred to more than the activity of philosophizing; it referred to "us," the collective historical subject of today; "What are *we* today?" "What are we in our actuality?" (1988, p. 145). Foucault's questions invite inquiries into the historicity of selfhood and the special (Oh! so special) place in our cultural life today of "selfhood" and "identity"—their enduring place as spiritual and moral projects in our cultures. Foucault's particular and influential line of inquiry concerned the exact history of our present self-attentiveness—the technologies that permit us to affect our bodies, souls, thoughts, relations, and actions and, in such a way, that we achieve authenticity, happiness, peace, and purity (1988, p. 18).

Until quite recently, it was the prevailing idea that culture merely provided the materials assimilated by a universal human subject. In fact, the overwhelming interest in the "study of Man" within anthropology derived from interest in the discovery of crosscultural similarities (Kleinman 1988, Ch. 2; Geertz 1983, Ch. 7). Only a minority of social scientists argued that languages and ideologies of selfhood—the distinct vocabularies of selfhood and the forms of self-experience and consciousness that these ideas produce in human beings—profoundly affect selfhood.[2]

The issue of the historicized self versus the universalized self points to one of the persistent tensions in social science since its inception—the tension between the *particularizing* and relativizing tendencies of social scientific methods and discourses and the *universalizing* thrust that so much of its work belies or explicitly avows. When considerations of the self are placed within these two consistent and conflicting tendencies, the conflict is between those who would affirm the transcultural nature of the self—*Culture merely provides the materials assimilated by a universal human subject*—and others, whose work seeks to particularize subjectivity and selfhood, focusing on the ways that *languages and ideologies of selfhood profoundly affect selfhood.*

In many ways, direct and circuitous, these opposing views have been linked to different ontologies of the human person and of reality itself: the true or authentic self as the foundation and unity of human existence, the precondition of consciousness and of Kant's Practical Reason versus the idea of self as history's complex product, where the ideals and interdicts of selfhood vary profoundly from age to age and from culture to culture, and where the objectifications of the self in and through knowledges and practices matter most. It is captured in the questions posed by a great ethnologist:

> Who knows even if this "category" [the person], which all of us here today believe to be well founded, will always be recognized as such? It was formed only for us, among us. Even its moral power—the sacred character of the human person—is questioned, not only everywhere in the East, where they have not attained our sciences, but even in some of the countries where the principle was discovered. We have a great wealth to defend; with us the Idea may disappear.
>
> (Mauss [1938] 1979, p. 90)[3]

The issue or the dilemma of a universalized versus a historicized self is not one confined to social scientists and social philosophers. It is a *cultural* dilemma, since it is communicated in our many and different discourses. What it communicates is our insistence, in the face of culture's power over us, that we are *more than* cultural artifacts. Our insistence that we are "free" tells us that we are "more than" culture's product; our relentless efforts at self-fashioning belie an anxiety that we are culture's mannequin. For others of us, this consciousness of construction—this "unbearable lightness" of a being without essence—drives us to insist that nature (and genes) still makes us who we are. But whatever we make of it—whether we flee from it or embrace it—*we know ourselves as a "construction" of culture.* This is who we are . . . today.

5

ENGENDERED KNOWLEDGE
Feminism and science

In societies like ours . . . "Truth" is centered on the form of scientific discourse
and the institutions which produce it . . . it is the issue of a whole political debate
and social confrontation.

(Michel Foucault)

PRELIMINARY CONSIDERATIONS

At the center, the very heart, of what we call "Western civilization" is the
twofold idea of science and reason: civilization's Enlightened Reason may,
indeed, represent more than any other idea its own progressive history and its
capacity to bring about a world free from prejudice and superstition. But it is
especially through the use of scientific knowledges and the technologies they
spawn that Western peoples have come to believe that they possess the capacity
to live better lives and in more humane conditions and to achieve the equality
they doubly claim as both the foundation and the hope of their democracies.
The perfectibility of the entire human race, particularly the hope of its freedom
from prejudice, domination, and brutality, has been—almost without inter-
ruption from the eighteenth century—inextricably bound up with the very
idea of science. Indeed, Hans-Georg Gadamer refers to this idea of perfect-
ability, of "self-formation or cultivation," as "perhaps the greatest idea of the
eighteenth century," giving Enlightened Reason "a fundamentally new content," and creating the very "atmosphere breathed by the human sciences of the
nineteenth century" (1975, p. 10). This "progressive" idea has inevitably
stemmed from the economic features of Western societies: industrial capitalism's requirement of change and movement and its consequent emphasis on
"the virtues of 'newness'" and inevitable progress (Wallerstein 1990, p. 37).
But the origins and development of the idea of progress are rooted just as much
in classical civilization's fascination with knowledge and its faith in "objective
knowledge" (Nisbet 1980).

The idea of scientific knowledge, which was so central to the legacy of
Western civilization and to the period of the eighteenth-century Enlightenment, conceived of itself as a project of all humanity—Kant's "humanity

85

come of age" or Diderot's depiction of the *philosophe* as humankind's universal guide. For there were no national boundaries to Enlightenment's "critical reason." Quite the contrary, their sciences would help all peoples and change the entire world, even in the face of the overwhelming obstacles of ignorance, slavery, and barbarism. This confident embrace of science as a progressive force for humankind's deliverance rested on the idea that scientific knowledge (itself a *universal* method) pursued universal laws whose discovery led all peoples toward their natural destiny. "The sole foundation for belief in the natural sciences," Condorcet claimed,

> is this idea, that the general laws directing the phenomena of the universe, known or unknown, are necessary and constant.... The progress of the sciences ensures the progress of the art of education, which in turn advances that of the sciences. This reciprocal influence whose activity is ceaselessly renewed, deserves to be seen as one of the most powerful and active causes working for the perfection of mankind.
>
> (Condorcet [1794] 1973, pp. 803, 805)

According to contemporary observers, these two all-pervasive ideas and their accompanying narratives—the liberation of humanity and the unity and universality of knowledge—provided the very life and spirit of our distinctive forms of collective morality, of our political unconscious, and of our national identities. In doing so, they have rendered our science a kind of eternal truth and human verity. Science as the practical embodiment of impersonal reason has, then, provided the West with our grandest and our most vital stories.

The *universalism* of science's methods and its objects—laws of nature, of Man, and of society—meant that science's ethos lay in its objective and impersonal character. Indeed, science represented impersonal reason in its fullest form. In ordinary terms, science's truths did not depend on the personal or social traits of the scientist—nation, religion, race. These were, in fact, deemed irrelevant to the scientific enterprise and inimical to its goals: "The imperative of universalism is rooted deep in the impersonal character of science" (Merton [1942] 1990, p. 69) and is compatible with the operations and standards of democratic societies. For both science and democratic governments uphold *in principle* the idea that particularism has no place as a criteria for either the pursuit of scientific truth or in matters of political justice. While a careful history and sociology of the "scientific tribe" (Clarke 1969) would undoubtedly reveal a diverse and complex set of ideas and practices about science's universal stance, including critiques by scientists themselves, *universalism has summarily defined what, in principle, science is.* At least until now.

For the last half-century the idea of a universal science has been ever so slowly but decisively challenged by intellectual movements and sociopolitical movements, which though remarkably different in most other respects, share a skepticism about the possibility and even the ideal of a general science of humankind with its rationalist assumptions about the application of science for human betterment. An assortment of intellectual developments, directed against positivism, has effectively undermined its place as the foundation of social philosophy and as the chosen method of social science. Hermeneuticists, structuralists and poststructuralists, deconstructionists, and culture theorists in a broad range of disciplines—anthropology and sociology, philosophy, literary studies, and history—offer competing models for disciplinary knowledge and practice. The models that they espouse, particularly that of the "text" and its interpretation or the model of "language" (understood through theories of rhetoric, representation, or discourse), highlight the constructed and even artificial character of their objects of investigation; as well, they draw attention to the problem of grasping the objects of all inquiries "objectively." In the terms of "interpretation theory," *understanding* something—be it human gesture, written sign, or written text—involves "a distinct and irreducible mode of intelligibility" (Ricoeur 1976, p. 72). Understanding differs from *explanation,* which has distinguished science's pursuit of causes through the discovery of laws and the accompanying idea of "reality" as something that stands on its own, that is, apart from our interpretation of it.

During the same period—roughly the last half-century—contemporary intellectual life has been beset with a crisis of rationality and what one philosopher-guide has identified as "the specter of relativism...hovering" behind and beneath these debates and dialogues (Bernstein 1983, pp. x–xi). The participants, he claims, have raised profoundly critical questions about the categories, distinctions, and biases that shaped our culture and our everyday lives since the seventeenth century. The anthropologist James Clifford (1986, p. 10), in his own assessment of the recent crisis of representation, concurs with respect to the historical significance of the current crisis: contemporary critiques have been directed against "the West's most confident, characteristic discourses." For the participants, the very idea of science and of a *universal knowledge* whose methods and structures grasp truths, terminate in objects, or uncover reality has become problematic or, in some quarters, suspect. In sharp contrast to the claim that scientific methods discover and describe an objective universe, these approaches argue that "reality" is relational, the quotation marks pointing to the relative and problematic status of what that reality is: what is real is to be grasped through its relationship to specific discourses or to "codes" or "conventions" of thinking and acting. And whereas, previously, scientific methods were employed to establish objectivity, today "objectivity" is seen as something discursively accomplished; both personal subjectivity and the authority of cultural accounts are even explored as "mutually enforcing fictions" (Clifford 1985).

As part of these developments—both articulating the relative and circumscribed contexts of knowing and disseminating this perspective even further—the concept of "culture" has come to the forefront of these discussions (Robertson 1992, Ch. 2). It might even be said that the uses of the concept have grown and gained momentum just as the convictions regarding the "tyranny of Method" (Bernstein 1983, p. xi) and the scientific enterprise have established themselves. "Culture," understood as the changing, tenuous, and thoroughly human and contingent ground of experience and knowledge, has operated as the category that represents what universal reason is not. The very idea of culture is eminently compatible with an approach that is "a more historically situated, nonalgorithmic, flexible understanding of human rationality, one which highlights the tacit dimension of human judgment and imagination and is sensitive to the unsuspected contingencies and genuine novelties encountered in particular situations" (Bernstein 1983, p. xi). "Culture" has enabled us to represent the pluralistic, contingent, and local features of our social existences, to stress difference over unity, to assert the idea of constructions over essences, to "wage war on totality" (Lyotard 1984, p. 82). In political terms, "culture" allows for world peoples to converse with their others, to think beyond their own origins, and to enter a realm where difference finds itself articulated (Bhabha 1994); "culture" enables us to speak across and between cultures at a time when a "global culture" is in the making (Featherstone 1990). "Culture" is also a construct through which Western capitalism comes to terms with the problem of "universalism" in the face of difference (viz., racism and sexism) and change (Wallerstein 1990).

Even in the social sciences, "culture" (both the concept and the theory) serves a larger need in our thinking, a broader function than as a mere tool for systematic inquiry. "Culture" is a "newly problematic object" (Clifford 1986, p. 3) of many disciplines, for it articulates our contemporary sense of the fluid, globally formed but locally grounded terrain of collective practices, particularly the prevailing forms of representation (images, symbols, ideas, discourses, texts). It also signifies the contemporary turn to everyday life, to the politics of meaning and signification, and to the prevailing metaphors in use in social science today—those of language and textuality. All of this is what "culture" and "cultural studies" represent (and re-present)—a kind of permanently "displaced" enterprise, like many of our world's peoples. In the words of one of cultural studies' most important spokespersons, cultural studies "holds theoretical and political questions in an ever irresolvable but permanent tension . . . [allowing] the one to irritate, bother, and disturb the other, without insisting on some final theoretical closure" (Hall 1992, p. 284).

Accordingly, we can speak of the "invention of culture," that is, its uses to interpret peoples, groups, and civilizations and not to represent them (Wagner 1981). We can construe this "invention of culture" as a *strategy* of some Western intellectuals whose preoccupations are with the "grounds of meaning and identity" and whose world makes it "increasingly difficult to attach human identity and meaning to a coherent 'culture' or 'language'" (Clifford 1988, p. 95). For them (and, perhaps, for others too), "culture" articulates the fragmentation of the "grand narratives" (Lyotard 1984) of Western civilization, of which rational science is its grandest.

But who and what deflated this grand narrative? Who or what rendered science something fabricated or constructed? How were rational science and its universalizing claims rendered improbable? How did we come to speak, as we do today, of a "culture of science?" The answers to these questions undoubtedly lie as much in the domain of social and political movements as they do in the intellectual developments of the last half-century. Although I will not take them up here, answers must also come from science itself, its self-critical and nondogmatic features, its responsiveness to social and cultural developments, and its skepticism concerning its autonomy vis-à-vis the sociopolitical context within which it works. All of these invite and promote a "culture of complaint" (Hughes 1993) even against itself.

For integral to the very idea of scientific objectivity is the idea of science as a self-correcting enterprise, inviting regular and systematic reinterpretations of its own methods and objects of study. Scientific rationality has, and can still, bring about the transformation of its own enterprise (Harding 1991, pp. 3–4). Scientific objectivity also includes standards of professional integrity that can serve to legitimate the scrutiny of scientists by scientists. In the infamous case of David Baltimore (the Rockefeller University scientist and Nobel laureate who refused to investigate allegations of faked research notes), the young scientist Margot O'Toole, who exposed the case, insisted that she was merely maintaining her commitment to scientific integrity (Hilts 1991; 1992), thereby drawing on the very idea of science to raise troubling questions about the validity of a senior scientist's work. Indeed, the scandalous features of this case derive from the public and professional recognition that Baltimore and his numerous and well-placed collegial supporters violated the very professional standards that he and they were expected to uphold: self-critical and systematic practices and procedures are, *in principle*, precisely what scientific methods claim to be. For this reason, examinations, such as this one, of science's critics will, of necessity, include scientists themselves who number among the ranks of science's critics (feminists, environmentalists, opponents of nuclear build-up, etc.).

Questions about who laid the groundwork for the important recent criticisms of science and its practice inevitably involve considerations about *what science is*: how science is not a thing, and surely not something univocal. Rather, science is something historically variable. As with any other central feature of industrial societies, science changes, as does its place in contemporary societies—such as its place in government, in war, in social policy and planning. As to science's critics, the extension of science's authority and its power in this half-century has certainly affected the rise of movements to oppose and to scrutinize science's practices. In the United States today, the number of scientists approaches 1 million and its share of the federal budget reaches $25 billion; in 1940 only about 200,000 scientists claimed 70 million in federal dollars (Hilts 1992). Formulated differently, the rate of growth for science has been far greater than the growth of national income (Rose and Rose 1969, p. 4). Thus the question of science's *legitimation* has been raised precisely during the period of science's expansion and increasing influence and power within the societies of late modernity. That extension of its functions has, in some ways, actually served to undermine its authority and credibility in society-at-large as an impartial, humane, and objective enterprise. But it should also be added that, in many important respects, despite the formidable challenge to science's practices, "the elephant has not even flicked its trunk or noticeably glanced" at its perturbators (Bleier 1986, p. 1). Whether or not this is of consequence will be an issue I will address later.

SCIENCE UNDER FIRE

Science's recent history has been marked by many and diverse movements of critics intent upon exposing its abuses and undermining its authority. In part, these movements represent the citizenry's attempt to grapple with and to hold someone accountable for the increasing dangers and risks of medical and technological developments: nuclear and chemical warfare, the environmental and chemical sources of pollution and disease, such destructive accidents to nature as oil spills, the hazards that accompany new medical treatments and surgeries. In fact, these movements of environmentalists, antinuclear groups, animal rights activists, and others have effectively exposed major frauds and abuses of scientific practices and effected changes in the treatment and experimental use of "human subjects" and other animals, the excessive use of drug treatments and therapies for institutionalized populations, abusive medical treatments of women, and the exploitation of workers and soldiers through their exposure to life-threatening chemicals and technologies.

For more than two decades, science's critics, especially the feminists, have presented a formidable opposition to the institutions of science and technology. Organized groups of women have launched their attacks on two fronts—political and intellectual. In the first place, they have demanded reforms in medical practices involving women as clients (birthing, breast and ovarian cancer diagnoses and treatments, abortion, surrogate motherhood, etc.). In the process, they claimed to speak for others marginalized by the institutions and establishments of medical practice as much as for themselves. Protests by women have also extended to the major institutions of law, politics, and social welfare. In the process, feminists and others have clearly had a hand in undermining science's reputation as a humanly progressive and universally directed enterprise. In the universities, feminist critics documented the exclusion of women from the sciences (see Rossi 1965 for an early statement; Rose 1986 and Hubbard 1990, Chs. 3–4, for a review and update), as well as from all the other leading fields of "knowledge production" in contemporary society (law, social policy and government, the academic professions, etc.). Women acting as individuals and within women's groups were also conspicuous in their active roles as leaders and effective as mobilizers in the American peace movement of the 1980s (Lofland 1993), as well as in the ecology and

90

environmental movements of the same period. Each of these focused their political attacks on the "imperialist" practices of U.S. and other Western scientific establishments: the state, in the case of the machinery and technology of nuclear warfare; multinational corporations aided by nation-states, in the case of the perpetrators of environmental waste and destruction.

Feminist critics

Those feminists whose principal places and audiences were the universities began their attacks on science and the scientific establishment by documenting the long-standing exclusion of women from all of the fields and professions represented by the universities. Feminists uncovered what can be summarily described as a "masculine bias" that went to the very concepts, theories, and methods of most academic disciplines: for example, early critical writings appeared in physics (Keller 1978; 1985); in philosophy (Harding and Hintikka 1983); in history (Janssen-Jurreit 1980); in psychology (Gilligan 1979; 1982; Sherif 1979); in sociology and social theory (Bart 1971; Bernard 1973; Smith 1987, see p. 22, n. 7). This body of research made clear that the sciences (science and engineering, excluding the social sciences) were by far more systematically exclusionary of women than the other disciplines (Rosser 1986; National Science Foundation 1982). With respect to the thousands of women who succeeded in breaking into the sciences, feminists documented women's long-standing and current segregated and low-status employment and under-recognition in their fields of endeavor (Weisstein 1977; *Signs* 1978; Vetter 1980; Rossiter 1982).

Studies also documented the widespread practice, until very recently, of the exclusion of women as research subjects in scientific studies. Equally important as this exclusion was the common practice of these studies to generalize their findings to both men and women. In medicine and in psychology, for example, this led to a systematic ignorance of developmental features and medical conditions peculiar to females. What we thought we knew about psychological and medical "human development" was, in effect, a knowledge of male development (Belenky *et al.* 1986). Practices such as these revealed a common-place "androcentric" perception, where men stood as the measure of all human beings, a perception that male scientists failed to perceive, just as they, almost without exception, had failed to generate systematic and unprejudicial knowledge about women's health and their bodies (Longino 1990, pp. 129ff.). Given the high rates of breast cancer and female heart disease, for example, relatively little was known about their etiology and treatments. The beginnings of the feminist critique of science began with these questions: "What is the basis of this ignorance about women?" "What is it about science—or about women—or about feminists—that explains the virtual absence of a feminist voice in the natural sciences?" (Bleier 1986, p. 1). "What is to be done about the situation of women in science" or about the "woman question in science" (Harding 1986, p.

9)? What has scientific knowledge-seeking meant, and what does it now mean, for women?

In most cases, documenting science's exclusion of women from the practice of science, however important in undermining the scientific claims of objectivity and universalism, did not, in itself, constitute a radical critique of science—that is, one that brought into question the foundational claims of the scientific enterprise, particularly its claims to scientific rationality. For however much the discriminatory practices against women were documented, this did not undermine science's claims to its universalism and objectivism. For the response to these practices could merely have been to correct them through fairer and more equitable practices—that is, by making unscientific science more scientific.

A far more thoroughgoing challenge to science followed in other and different kinds of feminist studies, particularly those that showed how scientific concepts and theories, such as in biology, immunology, and psychology, contained within them the historically and culturally based notions of the *legitimacy* of the historically subordinate status of women. For example, Bleier's (1984) work on biological theories and research was concerned with how biological science contributed to the elaboration of prevailing ideas about women's biological inferiority—ideas legitimating women's socially inferior status in Western civilization. Haraway (1989), Longino and Doell (1983), and Longino (1990) provided research that addressed how precisely "androcentric" and "sexist"[1] concepts and interpretations entered primatology and evolutionary theory and research practices (i.e., through concepts and hypotheses, in the actual research designs, and in the collection and interpretation of data). Haraway's work in the history of science (1989, Ch. 10; cf. Harding 1991, pp. 209–11; 1986, pp. 233–9) examined how both race and gender meanings of "civilized" and African peoples entered into primatology and how the primatology of different nations and cultures (e.g., Indian, Japanese, American) reflected different conceptions of nature and society. Haraway's work demonstrated how primatology's ideas could be read as part of particular national and cultural political discourses that served as legitimizing schemes of political domination (see Longino's 1990 discussion, pp. 209–14). These forms of research introduced a view of the objects of primatology—primates and their behavior—as sociocultural objects that served as "resources for appropriation" (Haraway 1991, p. 197). Or, to take the example of biology and evolutionary science and to use a different metaphor, the human bodies of males and females of different species served as spaces on which sociopolitical inscriptions could be written. "Nature," in Haraway's words, "is only the raw material of culture, appropriated, preserved, enslaved, exalted, or otherwise made flexible for disposal by culture" (1991, p. 98; cf. Angier 1994). However different her research methods, Hubbard (1990, Part II) also showed how in the fields of genetics and evolutionary processes, historically and culturally specific assumptions on human nature, human sexuality, and sexual difference were articulated and elaborated through scientific studies. "Nature is part of history and culture," Hubbard argued, "not the other way around." Hubbard (1990, p. 1) and Bleier (1984; 1986) have provided convincing reviews of the "sex differences" focus in biological studies of brain structure, hormones, and genes; both conclude that research does not provide empirical support for this long-standing scientific preoccupation. Hubbard also claims that the concept of "sex difference" itself is ineluctably political and moral, and linked to the domination of women and its legitimation. (Science's focus on "difference," she argues here, also has important legitimizing effects for race and class distinctions.)

Longino's thorough review (1990, Chs. 6–7; cf. Harding's 1986, Ch. 4, review of Longino and Doell 1983) of studies of sex differences in the fields of physical anthropology, physiological psychology, and endocrinology examines hypotheses (and their background assumptions) and data in order to identify central philosophical questions about scientific inquiry—specifically, how values and assumptions shape scientific inquiry. Her analysis of and conclusions about sex-differences research are distinctive, in several respects, from those of other critics. Relative to other feminist critics, Longino is a moderate who proposes a "contextual empiricism." She does not hold the view that the scientific method, including its focus on "difference," is inherently androcentric (although she regularly identifies androcentric and sexist assumptions in operation at various phases of scientific studies). Her "contextualist" method views science as an enterprise that incorporates into itself the ability and the requirement to examine assumptions and interests at work in scientific inquiries—both values of science itself ("constitutive" values), such as accuracy and predictability, and background assumptions (or "contextual" or socio-cultural values). While these latter often elude empirical assessment, they clearly provide the environment and ethos within which scientific work proceeds. Scientific practices and contextual values exist "in dynamic interaction" (Longino 1990, p. 5), and, in fact, "logical and cognitive structures of scientific inquiry require such interaction" (p. 185). Her portrayal of scientific practices still holds out (against other feminist critics) for the capacity of scientists and/or their audiences to reflexively examine how contextual values and interests—while, in principle, external to their investigations—actually operate at all levels of research and analysis (description, presentation, and interpretation of data). Yet, along with her sister critics, she rejects outright the idea and ideal of value-free science and proposes how a feminist science (as well as other politically committed scientific inquiries) can operate as a politically sensitive science (1990, Ch. 9). She also uses a revisionist notion of "ideology" that is entirely consistent with the prevailing views of other feminist critics: ideology no longer serves its long-standing function as the foil of scientific or philosophical knowledges. For ideologies operate throughout mainstream science, and "counterideologies" can be used to direct and to change existing science (1990, p. 187). Accordingly, ideologies now occupy their rightful place within science and direct the course of the "new" science.

My own interest in the works of the feminist critics is to assess what will likely be (and has been) the outcome (practical and theoretical) of their criticisms—and for whom. For myself, the answer to the question "For whom?" is of greatest import. While I will directly address this question at the conclusion of this chapter, I will begin by saying that the feminists' greatest impact—by no means inconsequential—is being felt within the universities. It is there that their *theoretical* argument (along with their supporting research) that *science is culture* has reverberated across the disciplines of the humanities and social sciences, opening up cross-disciplinary inquiries into the cultural foundations of knowledge-seeking and rationality. However vast the differences that separate the most important feminist critics (differences that occupy and trouble them more than their readers, I suspect), the feminist critics are similar in their insistence that *science be understood and examined as a thoroughly social and cultural activity*. I include here—listing the leading critics and their most characteristic positions—Sandra Harding's (1986) argument that a critical and self-reflective social science should be the model for all science, and that the natural sciences are best analyzed as part of social science (1991); Donna Haraway's conception of scientific knowledge as "situated knowledge" (1988; 1991, Ch. 9) that includes the idea of scientific knowledge as a truth-rhetoric, her particular use of Foucault's (1982) view of scientific objects as "constituted objects," and her insistence on "partial perspectives" over relativisms and holisms—each of these employing a radical "social constructionist" position; Helen Longino's view of science as a "social knowledge" where social values play an active and necessary role in its continual development; and Ruth Bleier's view of science as "a socially produced body of knowledge and a cultural institution" (1986, p. 2). Biology (Bleier's principal field of study) is a set of ideas and practices that reproduces and "naturalizes" the conventions of thought and feeling in the culture-at-large. Hilary Rose's (1986; 1994) sociological and "material theory" views scientific work as an important instance of the general division of sexual labor in society—a view that debunks the ideology of science as "above gender," a strategy particular to science of disavowing itself of culture, claiming itself a "culture of no culture" (1994, p. 2; cf. Aronowitz 1988). Dorothy Smith's contributions to a sociocultural theory of science (1987; 1990a; 1990b) consist of two decades of writings and research in which she examines social scientific and psychiatric knowledges as a vital part of the complex strategies for ruling, managing, and administering women's lives.

The science-as-culture perspective has also been important for both political and intellectual movements of science's critics. Politically, feminists and other critics of science—peace activists, antinuclear activists, and ecologists—launched social movements in the 1960s and 1970s that challenged the idea of the autonomy of science from sociocultural life, drawing attention to its practical and political links to the institutions of politics, business, and the military. These movements undoubtedly influenced how science has been construed in the popular mind, undermining, as they and others did, the long-standing view of science as a fundamentally neutral endeavor, separable—practically, politically, culturally—from its social and ideological environment. The claim of feminists, but also of the vast numbers of others engaged in challenging science and technology's destructive history and its future, was that scientific knowledges themselves—in physics, chemistry, biology—operated integrally with our markets, our forms of governance, and our institutions of war-making. The idea of science-as-culture was undoubtedly born of political movements such as these, that saw in the claim of science's "autonomy" an ideological deceit, an idea not far removed from the more fully elaborated one of science as particular historical and social formations—as epistemologies that function as "justificatory strategies" of the powerful, scientific discourses, which in their claims to objective knowledge, rationalize the beliefs of the powerful (Harding 1990, p. 87).

The idea of science-as-culture was also an idea in the air breathed by hosts of academics at about the same time. From a variety of disciplines and perspectives, analysts demonstrated that no knowledges are exempt from the operations of power and that any and all knowledges operate as *languages* (the preeminent cultural form). This means, *inter alia*, that, as with language, knowledges provide the structures and operations for all representations of reality. A leading argument—drawn principally from discourse analysis, which feminists have used—is that objects of knowledge are *constituted as objects of inquiry* under or within a system of descriptions—descriptions that already exist within a collective (sociocultural) context.[2] Drawing from the works of their contemporaries, particularly in literature and linguistics, as well as from the "strong program" in the sociology of science (Bloor 1991), the feminists systematized the idea of the congruence of science and all socio-cultural forms, texts, and practices. Science's "natural objects," they argued, already exist within sociocultural fields of interpretation in such a way that sociocultural values and ideologies operate in the very structuring of scientific inquiries and procedures; that is, cultural meanings (concerning nature, monogamy, womanhood, the body, etc.) operate as part of scientific inquiries. Indeed, how could it be otherwise? Scientific knowledge is something constructed out of a world already "known" and experienced *as something*; scientific knowledge-seeking presumes a cultural habitat in which science unfolds itself.

But objects are constituted in another sense, too: in the doing of science—in the work of scientists in laboratories—knowledge production is "constructive rather than descriptive": the *practice of science* can be examined by construing it as a *cultural activity in its own right*; "scientific objects are 'technically' manufactured in laboratories . . . symbolically and politically construed" (Knorr-Cetina 1993, p. 4). The objects of science—its facts, operations, and measurements—are, to borrow Thomas Kuhn's (1970, p. 126) phrase, "the collected with difficulty." They are neither "the given" of experience nor what is directly seen; they are "paradigm-determined." As to our "knowledge" of things perceived, our scientific perceptions are *educated* perceptions: "We have no direct access to what it is we know, no rules or generalizations with which to express this knowledge" (Kuhn 1970, p. 196).

Haraway's work (1991, Ch. 9), for example, draws from the work of, principally British, sociologists of scientific knowledge (Bruno Latour, Steve Woolgar *et al.*), whose work involves the study of science and technology through observational studies of sites of scientific production, especially laboratories. The sociologist of science Karin Knorr-Cetina (1993, p. 5) has described the theoretical significance of the laboratory in a way that makes clear how this approach opens up the "culture" of the laboratory, its informal and ordinary features:

> The significance of the notion of the laboratory lies not only in the fact that it has opened up this field of investigation and offered a cultural framework for plowing this field. It lies also in the fact that the laboratory itself has become a theoretical notion in our understanding of science. According to this perspective, the laboratory is the locus of mechanisms and processes which can be taken to account for the "success" of science ... these mechanisms and processes are non-methodological and mundane. They appear to have not much to do with a special scientific logic of procedure, with rationality, or with what is generally meant by "validation". . . . The laboratory is an "enhanced" environment which "improves upon" the natural order as experienced in everyday life in relation to the social order. How does this "improvement" come about? Laboratory studies suggest that it rests upon the *malleability* of natural objects ... objects are not fixed entities which have to be taken "as they are" ... laboratories rarely work with objects as they occur in nature ... they work with object-images or with their visual, auditory, electrical, etc. traces, with their components, their extractions, their "purified" versions.

Despite the objections of some feminist critics[3] to those engaged in the social study of science, there are many important points of agreement between them. Both groups adopt an explicitly cultural approach to science, with all that implies: a nominalist (*vs* essentialist) view of science as a complex sociohistorical formation ever changing itself and changed by its world; a view of science as a form of knowledge-production that is, in its most important aspects, comparable in its organization and practices to other forms of knowledge-production; a view of scientific methodology as involving complex rituals and activities that employ cultural categories, meanings, and symbols; a view of scientific work as a social activity constructed by discourse and power.

But the feminists offered something important and distinctive to the criticisms of science, extending the prevailing idea of science-as-culture and adding to it a political content of some consequence. As a cultural force and a discourse, they argued, science's categories and classificatory schemes, its problems, and its objects of inquiry operate as an ideological force, naturalizing the subjugation of women while, at the same time, rendering itself outside of culture and history and, thereby, exempt from social and cultural analysis (Harding 1986, Ch. 5; Rose 1994, p. 97). "The problem of what we are calling *ideological practices*," Dorothy Smith wrote, "is that they confine us to the conceptual level, suppressing the presence and working of the underlying relations they express" (1990a, p. 37). Accordingly, science's claims to universalism, neutrality, and objectivity are, in their effects, mystifications. What they effectively mystify—besides science's own specialized practices, its own rarefied modes of operation, its exclusionary practices and secret rites— are, precisely, its cultural operations. By highlighting the "hypocrisy and irrationality of [science's] universalistic claims in the face of overt and tacit discriminatory practices," feminism drew attention to science's mystifications (Harding 1991, p. 32).

If, as the feminists argue, scientific knowledge is best understood as a cultural formation, then science can be opened up and subjected to socio-historical inquiries. If science is a "social construct," then its construction and its constructors could be looked into. Such a logic served as an invitation for a whole host of cultural inquiries into scientific work, into the presuppositions of science's inquiries, its prevailing metaphors, its ruling methods and techniques, and the ways these were linked to economics, politics, and culture. Feminist scholars laid claim to the view that the idea of culture and its study, using "cultural science" methods (from sociology, anthropology, linguistics, literary theory, etc.), could be used to evaluate science. Science was no longer seen as a set of methods and practices that could only be scrutinized by itself and within its own standards of knowledge- and truth-production. Science was no longer culturally immune (Aronowitz 1988, p. viii). This claim of science's cultural status had its defenders in many academic quarters (e.g., from hermeneutics and critical theory, from philosophy and history of science) and provided a clear content for the critique of the prevailing orthodoxies of Western civilization and culture—rationality, objectivity, and universal knowledge-seeking. Science would no longer occupy its elevated place above (looking down on) "society," but would be deeply implicated in its political history.[4]

SEXING SCIENCE

The particular "feminist" agenda was to demonstrate precisely how scientific knowledges were "gendered" and *engendered*, the product of particular progenitive acts—indeed, same-sex acts, involving as it did only men as its producers. For if science was integral to the vast and complex world of "modern industrial society"—if it was a "social construct," or a social and cultural phenomenon—

then science was a *male* creation and collaboration and represented *their* own particular historical and political lives within modern industrial societies. Expressed in Virginia Woolf's aphorism, "Science it would seem is not sexless; she is a man, a father and infected too" ([1938] 1966, p. 139).

Science's "infection," as Woolf called it in *Three Guineas*, is a disease, rampant in the nineteenth century, transmitted especially to men in public places and professions ("we detected its presence in Whitehall, in the universities, in the Church"). The symptoms were painfully evident: strong "infantile" emotions and fixations aroused "by any suggestion that women be admitted" to their ranks. For the purposes of excusing and concealing these emotions, science (also infected), with Nature as its expert witness, "produced measurements to order," claiming that the female brain was even too small to be examined. And if, indeed, that brain could pass examinations, it was not a creative brain; nor could it bear responsibility, nor earn high salaries. "So science argued, so the professors agreed" . . . and so intoned the fathers together with the priests (Woolf [1938] 1966, pp. 127, 135–40).

While the genres of Woolf and the feminist critics differ markedly, their logic is strikingly similar. They view science as deeply implicated in the exclusionary strategies of men. For the findings contained in scientific treatises, in evolutionary doctrines, or in theories on "human development" confirm the natural superiority of men. In the idiom of feminist social science, science was a set of ruling practices, "conceptual practices" (Smith 1990a), through which women's natures, their bodies, and their psychologies were *produced* (Hubbard *et al.* 1982). Indeed, given science's preeminent place within industrial civilization, science was *the most masculine form of knowledge*—abstract, objective, authoritative (Farganis 1986, p. 185); the very phrase "man scientist" was redundant (Harding 1991, p. 20). Declarations such as these were not only the property of feminists. Thomas Kuhn had concluded his 1969 "Postscript" to his classic treatise on science's history with a remarkably similar dictum, asserting that if scientific knowledge "is intrinsically the common property of a group . . . to understand it we shall need to know the special characteristics of the groups that create and use it" (Kuhn 1970, p. 210).

Science's very impersonality and abstractness, it was argued, reflected and expressed the experience of dominant classes of men in Western bourgeois society (e.g., Bordo 1987; Keller 1985; Merchant 1980; Rose 1983; Rose and Rose 1979). But these masculine dispositions also (and not incidentally) served to promulgate the privileged and protected positions of science and scientists. For example, in her essay "Women's Nature and Scientific Objectivity" (1981), Elizabeth Fee argued that the prevailing dichotomies of Western culture—reason/emotion, objectivity/subjectivity, culture/nature, public/private—have simultaneously served to ideologize the dominance of men as rulers in industrially based societies, to legitimate the place of science as "outside" of culture and politics, and to circumscribe women within positions and places appropriate to their female natures. "The identification of man as the knowing mind and woman as his connection to nature has been a continuing theme in Western culture." Women and human reproduction are consigned to the sphere of the "natural," while other human activities (and men) are assigned to the sphere of the "social" (Fee 1986, p. 44). Men's control over the production of scientific knowledges and discourses was inextricably part of their social and political domination as well as their power over women. Science was not only *what* men controlled, it was *how* they controlled. Through its knowledges one could discover *whom* men controlled.

Hilary Rose's recent work has traced how feminist research agendas shifted from their early concerns with the exclusion of women from science to the view of "women as produced by science," referring to scholarship that "drew on the concept of gender to illuminate a double process of a gendered science produced by a gendered knowledge production system" (Rose 1994, p. 18). Actually, these two agendas are closely related. For, as the feminists argued, the exclusion of women from science was something accomplished discursively inasmuch as scientific knowledges construed women in particular ways, as outside ("beneath," "incapable of," etc.) polity, rationality, and authority. This is particularly evident in the sciences of biology and psychology, where women's dependency and subordination were scientifically "confirmed" in innumerable ways (Hrdy 1981; Hubbard *et al.* 1979; Smith 1990a, Chs. 5–7; Broverman *et al.* 1970).

Women's "incapacities" were being studied as *scientifically constructed incapacities*. This does *not* mean that these incapacities were scientific fictions. It meant that within scientific discourses, *especially*, women had discovered their truest and most consequential incapacities vis-à-vis men. For one of the special functions of scientific discourses, be they medical, psychiatric, or belonging to an academic discipline, is to show women their greatest failings and vulnerabilities *as women*—to name and to map their mental shortcomings, their special pathologies, their physical excesses, or just their natural inabilities.

Dorothy Smith has called our attention to the "alienation of utterance," when women become "aware of modes of speaking, writing, and thinking" that take their powers of expression away from them even as they use them (Smith 1990a, pp. 199–200). Somewhat like the servant Stevens (in the film *The Remains of the Day*), whose appalling ignorance of public affairs confirms the view of his master's guest that Stevens and his ilk are ill-suited for self-governing. In fact, their lives of servitude and service to their masters, and the ignorance and humble dispositions these breed, are indisputable proof of their political incapacities. The parallel I am drawing here is between the discourses of "masters" (science, in the case of women) that implicate subordinate groups in their own subordination, tripping them up in ways that manage to validate their masters' convictions of their natures.

The psychologist Carol Gilligan has also pointed to something similar in the *silence of women* (1982, p. 173): "As we have listened for centuries to the voices of men and the theories of [psychological] development that their

99

experience informs, so we have come more recently to notice not only the silence of women but the difficulty of hearing what they say when they speak." Living in a world where they and their experiences are devalued, women's halting voices (like those of the servant Stevens) betray their own sense of mistrust in themselves, a mistrust born out of their habit of silence.

The metaphor of "voice"—captured in the phrases "speaking up," "being silenced," "having no voice," "finding one's voice" (Belenky *et al.*, 1986, p. 18)—has been the prevailing one for feminists writing in fields as diverse as history (Lerner 1986), psychology (Gilligan 1982), and poetry (Rich 1977). This very silence points to the active exclusion of women from the production of the prevailing and authoritative knowledges of Western civilization (law, science, medicine), as well as its rule. Of all the significant implications of this exclusion or this silencing of women, feminist writers have elaborated two in particular.

First, women's marginal status in the production of our civilization—in the making of science, technology, government, artistic and literary accomplishments—has effectively served to validate the claim of women's inferiority and, thereby, to legitimate their subordination. For women have nothing of their own ("no past, no history, no religion," Simone de Beauvoir wrote in *The Second Sex*), nothing with which to validate themselves and their own abilities and accomplishments. The idea of "discovering" or of "creating" their own history (the theoretical implications of these terms can differ widely) formed the centerpiece of Gerda Lerner's now classic *The Creation of Patriarchy* (1986), arguing that the writing of women's history is indispensable for changing their subordinate status. Without a history to show women their place within societies and civilizations, they have no alternatives; nothing—no history of themselves and their abilities—from which to draw in their attempt to assert themselves and to claim their place alongside men. As long as a woman's dialogues remain dialogues with the systems of great men, "the source of new insight is closed to her," and the impetus to actively insert herself in history is lost. For within these symbol systems of great men, "woman—as a concept, a collective entity, an individual—is marginal or subsumed" (Lerner 1986, p. 227).

These ideas are, of course, the same ideas and strategies of other groups today who in their urgency to uncover and to write their own achievements as a people are doing so in order to assert their rightful places in history and in world civilization. The same political reasoning applies: without a productive role in making history, without a record of accomplishments (as well as records of their oppression by others), their own political demands lack import.

Second, the feminist critics argue that their own project of rewriting women's history, as in the case of men's, draws from their own experiences and sociopolitical lives. Women's history, it is argued, will inevitably articulate a history out of their own collective experiences and will uncover those individual and collective accomplishments that were "lost" or devalued as part of their subordination and oppression. Aronowitz (1990, pp. 312–13) finds in the feminists' idea of being marginal to written history a thoroughly *cultural* political notion. For it asserts as the principal exclusionary form and force that of language and discourse: "women are the absence in the text of public discourse." Thus, he underscores, in his own commentary on feminist critics, that the *absence* of women in public discourses is not so much *expressive of their exclusion*, as it is *constitutive* of it, and it is thereby vital to overcome it in overcoming male supremacy.

The feminist theme of "finding a voice" means that they will speak out of their own collective experiences *as women*—that they will render these experiences as a valid way to "enter history," by speaking from their own standpoint and not men's: "[W]e already know that woman's mind, at last unfettered after so many millennia, will have its share in providing vision, order, solutions. Women at long last are demanding, as men did in the Renaissance, the right to explain, the right to define" (Lerner 1986, p. 229).

FEMINIST SCIENCE

The project of defining what science can become when science is placed in the hands and minds and hearts of women has occupied feminist critics since the 1980s. What has been called "women's standpoint," or the articulation of a feminist world view or feminist perspective based on the collective experiences of women, has been the centerpiece of feminist writings across the disciplines. Early statements by Dorothy Smith (1987), Hilary Rose (1983), and Nancy Hartsock (1983) were particularly important, exploring the possibilities for a distinctly "feminist science" that was grounded in the sociopolitical positions and social experiences of women—an "interested" or politically engaged science committed to understanding the world from the position of sub-jugated or marginalized peoples. Feminist science was a "successor science" in that its aim was to reconstruct Enlightenment science's project of liberating humanity, while challenging Enlightenment's claims to establish a "pure" Reason, free from the encumbrances of material life and social location. In the words of Harding (1991, p. 121), feminism's "successor science" uses "women's lives as grounds to criticize the dominant knowledge claims, which have been based primarily in the lives of men in the dominant races, classes, and cultures." Its goal is not "ideological" in the narrow meaning of this term. For the feminists have moved away from a critique of science-as-ideology to a critique of science-as-culture. (See my interpretation of ideology as culture in Chapter 2 of this book.) Their goal is to maximize and to strengthen the objectivity of scientific knowledge, "overcoming excessive reliance on dis-tinctively masculine lives and making use also of women's lives as origins for scientific problematics, sources of scientific evidence, and checks against the validity of knowledge claims" (Harding 1991, pp. 122–3; cf. Harding 1993a; 1993b; Rose 1994, pp. 93–6).

101

The issues surrounding the possibility of a feminist science opened up lengthy and labored epistemological inquiries regarding what a feminist "successor science" could mean, particularly in the face of postmodernist critiques of empiricist science and, indeed, of all "master narratives" (e.g., Nicholson 1990; Alcoff and Porter 1993). The feminist "standpoint theorists" found themselves in prolonged debates with feminists aligned with post-modernism, who questioned the very idea of a "feminist standpoint" or a "feminist science," as well as with others who challenged the very notion of their apparent claims to speak for *all* feminists, for *all* women. Was there, for example, such a thing as a world view or a knowledge distinctive to women? Didn't such a claim rest on "essentialist" notions, which defied the very social and historical contexts from which feminist theory drew? Wasn't the idea of a universal feminist standpoint grounded in a theory of women's essential nature, including their bodily natures? Could any single group of women be "prioritized" or claim "epistemic privilege" without subordinating others?[5] And so forth. (See the discussions in Rose 1994, Chs. 1–2; Longino 1990, Ch. 9; Harding 1991, Chs. 5 and 12; Harding 1986, Ch. 6.)

The debates on these questions have been extensive and passionate, involving as they have feminists with large personal and intellectual (and career) stakes in the terms and outcomes of these issues.[6] A vital issue in these debates is whether or not to invest effort and ink on a new science and a "stronger" or more inclusive objectivity (standpoint theory), or whether to stand in opposition to any and all universalizing discourses (science, reason, truth, objectivity), while promoting the value of multiple voices, as well as a complex "matrix of domination" (Collins 1990), and drawing attention to the "discourse" of science as a power/knowledge (postmodernism). Linda Nicholson (1990, p. 8) points out, and I agree, that for some feminists the troubling issue is whether the very category of gender will "survive the postmodern critique," its relentless relativism, its hostility to theory, and its suspicion of absolutes.

While I share Nicholson's concern with the survival of "gender" (the concept), I find it a concern that is entirely an academic one, since in the world-at-large (rather than the university-as-world) the concept of gender, along with that of race and, less so, ethnicity,[7] have swiftly taken up residence in the firmer quarters of the United State's *conscience collective*, as the unques-tioned grounds of one's social and political identity, differentiating each of us—man/woman, or whatever; black/white, or whatever—profoundly and inescapably. This is not to say that consciousness of gender and of race and their power as *représentations collectives* (to extend the allusion to Durkheim) have marched hand in hand with a growing social and political equality. There is, in fact, considerable evidence to support the view of the persistence of sexism (confining my remarks here to "gender") in public opinion, in collective sentiment, in the popular culture, in institutions of religion, in the workplace, and so forth. However, the *social reality of gender*—as a powerful collective category and a social fact that has entered our political lives, our professional discourse (scientific, medical, legal, etc.), and our everyday discursive lives—is undisputed. The collective awareness of the distinct sociocultural roles of men and women, of sexual "stereotypes," of "sexual harassment," and so on, is a powerful contemporary social fact. Wherever one stands on the value of that fact, it is a fact all the same.

SCIENCE-AS-CULTURE: AN ASSESSMENT

"Gender is a category born of culture" (Gergen 1991, p. 143). Its place in politics and public opinion has been, undoubtedly, the effect of feminist movements to change public consciousness in order to effectively attain social and political rights. But the conditions for that movement to effectively accomplish this can be found in cultural changes—changes in knowledges, technologies, literacy—far broader than the women's movement itself. Take the public consciousness of "gender" and "race," which I discuss above. Their effectiveness as social categories or collective representations were the effect of large and complex social processes: among them, the increased literacy of our populations and the dissemination of the modern sciences and disciplines (sociology, psychology) into common parlance and mental structures, the secularization of language and world view, as well as the effects of political movements (civil rights, feminism) on the popular consciousness.

From the long view (Braudel's *histoire de la longue durée*), "gender" and "race" were highly improbable ideas, unthinkable for centuries on end. The long and remarkably tenacious view was that to be male/female, black/white (the formulations are our own) were matters of "nature" or "fate," not "culture," unchanging biological facts; the unquestioned inferiority of women and blacks were facts of inferior brain capacity, moral weakness, and more. The "liberation" of women from what Lawrence Stone (1994) calls "two millennia of near slavery" occurred only in this century; women's equal opportunities for education are also only a century old. "Nothing," Stone observes, "is more striking than [women's] systematic deprivation of education." In a relatively short time, that education has served as both a condition for women's political and social emancipation, as well as an effect of that growing emancipation.

The liberation of women, then, coincided with movements and changes— in science, literacy, the rationalization of social life—that effectively brought into view the powerful reality of culture or the *fact* of culture in the production and maintenance of matters previously deemed utterly and inescapably "natural." For women, the idea of culture was inextricably part of their emancipation, serving effectively as a *strategy* for their emancipation, since changing the conditions of their subordination required the notion that sexual differences were culturally based ("gender"). Of course, historians of modernity might correctly point out that "culture" has been on our minds for some time now, at least since Europe's "discovery," throughout the sixteenth

103

century, of world civilizations (Anderson 1991, pp. 68–9; cf. Gay 1969, Ch. 7), and since the phenomenon of "pluralism" (Berger *et al.* 1973) in matters of religion, race, and nationality undermined the universalism of medieval civilization. But throughout this century, the *idea of culture* has become not only the province of intellectuals and academics, but a feature of a common world view, and an idea used in ordinary speech. In order for the idea of culture to gain the momentum that it has and in so brief a span in years, it is likely that it required the powerful impetus of a set of political movements: egalitarian movements seeking rights for women, for "ethnicities," and for all races. As Max Weber so often observed, ideas are powerless unless they are linked to a group's material interests. "Ideas are discredited in the face of history unless they point in the direction of conduct that various interests promote" (Gerth and Mills 1946, pp. 62–3).

If there is any single idea that has and can effectively change social institutions, indeed the very social fabric itself, it is that of "culture." Of course the social fabric has already been changed if the idea of "culture" is able to take root and to flourish, particularly its central image that *a society is something produced*. The revolutionary nature of this idea is perhaps best grasped today set against the rising tide of fundamentalisms or countermodernisms on the global scene. The idea of culture has been integral to modernity itself and to its pursuit of an Enlightened humanity, but it is, as Hilary Rose (1994, p. 238) has also observed, "deeply subversive" when used to define any authoritative body of knowledge as socially shaped. It is the "recognition" of its subversiveness that undoubtedly accounts, in part, for the brutal militancies of fundamentalisms in today's world. For feminist movements that arise amidst fundamentalist peoples, the combination can be particularly deadly.[8]

Despite the social transformations—modernization, secularization, democratization—that the idea of culture has both expressed and transmitted since its "discovery" in about the sixteenth century, the idea of science-as-culture was surely an improbable idea until very recently. The idea that science is no more (and no less) a "construction" than other things, suggests that it was "hammered together in some place to some purpose ... like everything else cultural. ... If knowledge is made, its making can be looked into" (Geertz 1990, p. 19).

The idea of science-as-culture radically undercuts Enlightenment's hope for a universal science, Condorcet's progressive hope for the "perfection of mankind," and replaces it with a worldly and political enterprise whose methods and truths—because they are "hammered together" by mere (mostly male) mortals—have become increasingly contentious. Their contentiousness is surely a function of science's increasing capacity, with its increasing power, to create havoc in our lives and in our environments. Science's critics have recognized that their enemy is a formidable one and that science's authority and legitimacy are unparalleled. Thus Foucault's (1980b, pp. 131–3) observations regarding the "political economy" of truth:

In societies like ours... "Truth" is centered on the form of scientific discourse and the institutions which produce it; it is subject to constant economic and political incitement... it is the object, under diverse forms, of immense diffusion and consumption... it is produced and transmitted under the control, dominant if not exclusive, of a few great political and economic apparatuses (university, army, writing, media)... it is the issue of a whole political debate and social confrontation.... The essential political problem for the intellectual is not to criticise the ideological contents supposedly linked to science... but that of ascertaining the possibility of constituting a new politics of truth.

The feminists have recognized that their most important achievement will be a new "feminist science" carved out of their struggle to compete in the production of truth. It is *their* struggle; it is for them, the "sisterhood." Among the many things it is, it is a struggle for control over the most formidable and consequential configurations of our world—science, technology, medicine, and their "apparatuses" (from universities to war rooms, from clinics to laboratories). The past struggles for the vote, for temperance, for birth control, for the right to work and to fight wars, and even for legalized abortion, pale in the face of the struggle of women to make science in a world where science is power. That this struggle is seen as a means of human and social liberation is striking in its evocation of our Enlightened forebears. Although the speakers and their speech might appall him, the feminist "hope for transformative knowledge" is a quest Condorcet would recognize.

EPILOGUE
Knowledge as culture

The work of sociology is a tradition of inquiry. With disconcerting literalism, this notion, which we discussed in Chapter 1, was dramatized for me when, as a graduate student in the 1970s, I discovered that the text of Mannheim's *Ideology and Utopia* that my teacher was consulting with me had been Mannheim's own copy, given to my teacher by Mannheim and liberally sprinkled with Mannheim's own annotations.

Sociology is a tradition of inquiry of modernity. Since its inception, Western social science has been inextricably linked to modernity, whether supportive or critical of its distinctive social formations. And in new and future phases of modernity—whether we call it "post-" or "high-modernity"— our discipline will continue to reflect and shape its development.

Sociology is a tradition of inquiry that is inherently revisionist; like society, which it studies, it achieves its present by continual reassessment of its past.

This book was written in the spirit of such a revisionism, both to address the needs of our discipline at century's end and to address our continuing task of revisiting and revising its persistent themes and concerns. My particular concerns are thus directed toward the present and the future, for I contend that the modern classics speak to us now. Such was the claim of Marshall Berman's study of modernism (1982). "Going back can be a way of going forward," he wrote; "remembering the modernisms of the 19th Century can help us gain the vision and courage to create the modernisms of the 21st" (p. 36). In 1992, Berman added: "I hoped to take social thought back to the future" (1992, p. 14). If he is right, and I think he is, recent intellectual movements, such as structuralism and poststructuralism, actually re-present, rather than leave behind, many of modernism's most urgent concerns and crises—at least, modernism at its best, attuned to the living context of its own ideas.

In each of the preceding chapters, the key ideas of the sociology of knowledge—ideology, structure, culture, human agency, the social self—have been reexamined in light of today. The purpose of this task was to raise the question of the adequacy of sociology's concepts and methods for grasping and for understanding today's world-in-transition, questioning whether the development and refinement of our concepts have kept pace with the changing social

106

and political landscape, with the changing world-system, its global culture, what some call the "internationalization of daily life," affecting its people and its classes as much as its commodities and cultural forms, its rational ethos transforming not only material life but minds and souls as well.

Surely one of the singular insights of the sociology of knowledge for social scientific inquiry is to be found in its claim that social life does not stop at the "doors" of our being, but passes into the chambers of our minds and our psyches, and insinuates itself even into the domain of spoken and unspoken thoughts and desires. Social life is not an aspect, but the environment of human being. The sociology of knowledge has always scrutinized the collective life of ideas, meanings, images, and symbols—those things most central to "society" and "human being." This is undoubtedly why it is a field of study that those outside of social science, those working in the humanities—philosophers, literary critics, theologians—have regularly drawn from. This was not always the case. For the sociology of knowledge—if we can judge by the responses of its earliest critics—once provided a considerable threat to both the humanities and the sciences.[1] More recently, for only about four decades now, the "social" and the "cultural" are seen as inextricably part of all knowledges. Disciplines outside of social science, from the study of literature and biology to that of ethics, have grown accustomed to using premises that Karl Mannheim and Max Scheler fought to establish: all aspects of human being and knowing are *situated*; thought and action form a unity; a society's intellectual developments cannot be divorced from its concrete historical and social contexts.

In my view, however, the lasting value (for now) of the sociology of knowledge is its capacity to draw attention to itself as part of its own inquiry: to enable us to scrutinize the current "turn to culture," both in society and in social science; to grasp—with more than an ounce of critical detachment—the effects that social scientific ideas and methods have on contemporary life; to ask how knowledge of culture and its operations can operate as a form of domination, since it is a resource from which many peoples are excluded. In its capacity to draw attention to its own operations, the sociology of knowledge claims that social scientific knowledge—as with all knowledges—*is* culture.

But what precisely does this academic formula mean? Throughout this book, I have attempted to examine what it means, using some of the major traditions of social theory to illuminate the condition of knowledge in our world today: Marxist social theory (Chapter 2), French sociology and anthropology (Chapter 3), and American pragmatism (Chapter 4). Various contemporary feminisms (Chapter 5) make up some of the newest body of work that addresses the topic of knowledge—drawing from, while substantially reconceiving, ideas from Marxism, sociology of knowledge and science, and poststructuralism. Today, each of these disparate "interpretive communities"[2] has placed the concept of "culture" in the forefront of these discussions. The reason for this "cultural turn" (Robertson 1992, Ch. 2) is itself a topic of interest, especially for the sociologist of knowledge. The postmodern world is now preoccupied with forms of signification (language, text, discourse, etc.), which, as Robertson notes (p. 32), the works of sociology that came after the classical period, roughly from the 1920s to the 1950s, largely neglected.

Yet, is it any surprise that the older ways of thinking about "base" and "superstructure" have changed rapidly and unalterably in this half-century? We live in a world almost overwhelmed by its own inventiveness, its own artificiality. Our realities exist in transmission—on screens and cables—and our sense is that those who possess and control knowledges and images and sounds effectively control our realities. Material life, as we understand it today, has become inescapably semiotic; we consume products that serve as signs of things and, more importantly, of ourselves. Our world of things exists more to communicate, to "say something," than to serve a practical need or function. As theories of discourse have gained ascendency in the academy, talk . . . talk . . . talk hounds us in daily life. People, led by the "talk shows" of radio and television, never seem to stop talking. In our time are we witnessing the death of conversation by talk? "Culture" also serves to account for our growing sense of "construction" and "difference" in a world that "whatever it is, is no longer One" (Lemert 1994, p. 146).

The current interest in culture grows out of our consciousness of world peoples and nations ("globalization") as well as the active dissemination and exchange of knowledge and information about world peoples among themselves. The use of the concept of "culture" in print and broadcast journalism educates us further into the real, yet remarkably elusive, fact of culture.[3] In the United States today we hear of the "culture of the military," the "culture of Washington, D.C.," "gay culture," and so forth. These popular usages both articulate and disseminate further people's consciousness of culture as the relative and shifting grounds of meaning and value. For to grasp something *as culture*, or as part of culture, is to grant to it an *artificial* status: humankind in all its various colors, shapes, and sizes is the supreme artificer of its world (culture) and of itself. To see culture as artificial and society as a human artifact has always been integral to social science, to its critical and detached perspectives and practices (Clifford 1988, p. 199; Stark 1980, p. 22). But what is relatively new is that these ideas are quickly becoming common coinage, brought about by the increased literacy of peoples and their acculturation by modern discourses and disciplines, the secularization of language and world view, and the effects of these on public opinion and popular culture. "Culture" no longer marks off the West from the non-West. It is now about us, too (Geertz 1995, Ch. 3), articulating our sense of the fluid, contingent, and local field of collective life and thought.

To assert that *knowledge is culture*, a claim that draws together the disparate theories presented in this book, is to insist that various bodies of knowledge, such as those of the natural sciences or the social sciences, operate *within* culture—that they contain and transmit and create cultural dispositions, meanings, and categories. It also means that all knowledges, whatever else they do, operate as systems of meaning; that they provide categories and conceptions that enable their users to understand their worlds *as something* (Percy 1958).

That knowledges can be profoundly consequential, particularly in their ability to frame the ways that persons, events, images, and goods come to be perceived, is not solely an academic theory. It is registered today on our collective consciousness and is a sign of the reflexive character of consciousness produced by modernization (Giddens 1990). Battles over culture and morality in the United States today grow out of precisely this recognition. Knowledges, particularly those of "interest groups" but also those produced by technicians and specialists, can contain and transmit all manner of values and judgments: Whose texts will be used to teach our children? Who has the right to educate them about sex? Knowledges produced by educators and publishers are "politicized," viewed as interest-based, and indeed this is often the case. In other domains, too, such as the courts, the knowledges of "expert witnesses" carry weight in the presentation of a case, even though they are also viewed as part of a partisan legal strategy. Jurors, hand-picked by lawyers to render particular verdicts, deal out jury knowledge—a mystifying, and, it would appear, mystic, knowledge of unparalleled authority. In each of these cases, the recognition that knowledges are partisan, or inescapably "local," serves neither to undermine their effects nor their authority.

Undoubtedly one of the foremost developments on the knowledge front has come from social and political movements of science's critics, both inside and outside the academy: feminists, environmentalists, opponents of nuclear build-up, veterans suffering from the effects of chemical warfare, defenders of animals from exploitative practices by industries and medical science. Each in its own way has contributed to the view that science—the institution once seen as standing well outside and above society—is itself a thoroughly social and human enterprise. Feminist critics within the academy, sharing the same institutional domain as scientists themselves, documented the long-standing exclusion of women from science and uncovered biases that went to the very concepts and theories of fields as diverse as physics, psychology, and engineering (Chapter 5).

The legacy the feminists left us, captured in the phrase *science is culture*, is an idea—at once original yet evocative of Foucault's genealogy of disciplinary practices—that the exclusion of women from science was something accomplished discursively. The idea of the natural superiority of men was not a mere reflection of social forms of subordination (as Marx claimed), but something *produced* through scientific representations and practices. Marginality and subordination are conditions *lived* by social actors. But they are also inscribed in categories, classifications, texts, and treatises. These cultural forms do not follow upon the "structures" of class and material life. Cultures circumscribe and situate people's lives: groups, classes, entire societies are the effects of a variety of "discursive formations" (Foucault) or complex networks and "apparatuses" (Althusser). "Ruling" and "governing" are not solely or even

109

principally a matter of either economics or politics. They are integral to *a total way of life*, precisely the phrase used by Kluckhohn (following E. B. Tylor's "most complex whole") to define "culture."[4]

Today, this idea of culture as unified and integrated has undergone criticism and revision within anthropology. Yet it contains the contemporary insight that every facet of a "social order"—itself a phenomenon produced and achieved—is something *meaningful*, something that can serve as a mode of signification, whether Gods, objects of adornment, money, sentiments, human gestures, or our garbage. Thus we can "read" so much of nineteenth-century "bourgeois culture," not only through the bourgeoisie's "'sublime' theories about the 'essence' of history and the state" (Lukács [1911] 1968, p. 66), but also through their "tender passions" and anxieties, their consciences and their racism (Gay 1984; 1986; 1993). Puritanism, Max Weber argued, was a worldly vision and form of intense religiosity—an ethos that Weber himself tried to capture through the commercial ventures of seventeenth-century capitalists, as well as by looking at Rembrandt's *Saul and David*, a work brimming with "the powerful influence of Puritan emotions" (Weber [1904–5] 1958, p. 273, n. 66). These are exemplifications of cultural sociology and entail uncovering the diverse meanings and messages of customs and values, artwork and dreamwork, and listening to the voices and the silences of past and present. Among cultural sociology's central tenets is that no artifact is meaningless—even the most practical instruments of our civilization have been used to speak, to dream, and to imagine. The census, the map, and the museum, Anderson (1991, p. 164) argues, were the institutions that "profoundly shaped the way in which the colonial state imagined its dominion—the nature of the human beings it rules, the geography of its domain, and the legitimacy of its ancestry."

Knowledges, as with any cultural artifact, do *more* than they purport to do. Many of the contributions to contemporary cultural studies have occupied themselves with this "more," arguing that science, law, and theology, for example, function as "discursive formations," as much in the business of ruling and marginalizing peoples as they dispense the knowledges that they own up to. While this perspective is one that we cannot shrink from, contemporary studies of culture have left us a legacy more unsettling in its main features. For the "more" that knowledges do and say is not principally a kind of lie; nor is it an impurity of which we can rid ourselves. As cultural (read *semiotic*) phenomena, knowledges are burdened with presuppositions derived from our cultures. In the practice of science, medicine, journalism, law, or social science, our authority as producers of knowledge can no longer be derived from our freedom from culture. On the contrary, those of us who engage in knowledge-production of these kinds are, in fact, *producers of culture*. This does not mean that all knowledges are *ex equo*, nor that all knowledges are ideological, in the classical Marxist sense of "false consciousness," nor that they must necessarily be ideological in any sense (see my discussion of ideology in Chapter 2). But it does impose on academics and professionals—to use an example close to me—a rather different sense of "vocation" than that described by Max Weber.

Today, in the university classroom, I can no longer limit myself to the instruction of my students into the ideas and methods of social science. I must also educate them about the operations of culture and about social science as part of culture. This entails, among other things, drawing attention to the ways that it and other bodies of knowledge reconfigure their societies and themselves, sometimes in ways that divest them of the identities and loyalties that they brought with them to school. The practice of social science also requires the cultivation of a trait of twentieth-century culture—one probably born of our sociology and anthropology—of being in culture while scrutinizing it.

Yet I remain committed to social science as a thoroughly liberal and liberating *habit of mind*, one that seeks out the complex origins and understandings of our contemporary worlds. And I am certain, in the dispensing of social scientific knowledge, of its value for my students, if for no other reason than the fact that it informs them about the circumstances that inevitably shape their lives. But, as I perform these operations, I know and they know that what I say and teach is not the final word. *Situated knowledges* are, by their nature, unfinished. But that is the character of all things human and alive.

NOTES

INTRODUCTION: THE SOCIOLOGY OF KNOWLEDGE AND CULTURE

1 For a discussion of the pragmatist features of classical sociology and sociology of knowledge, see Werner Stark ([1958] 1991, pp. 307ff.) and Kenneth Stikkers's (1980) introduction to Max Scheler's *Problems of a Sociology of Knowledge*.
2 I am citing Kenneth Thompson's (1986) discussion of neo-Durkheimian theories, including those of Benedict Anderson and Bernard Lacroix.
3 The term is borrowed from Mannheim's (1936) extensive "Preliminary Approach . . ." to the sociology of knowledge, especially pp. 45ff.

1 WHAT IS KNOWLEDGE?

1 Swidler and Arditi (1994, p. 306) use the same phrase as I do, "the new sociology of knowledge," and while certain points of their discussion overlap with my own, they designate as *knowledge* "cultural elements that are more conscious, more explicitly linked to specific institutional arenas, and more historically variable."

2 TRUE AND FALSE KNOWLEDGES: THE MARXIST TRADITION

1 An earlier and shorter version of this chapter was published as "The Uncertain Future of Ideology: Rereading Marx," a special issue of *The Sociological Quarterly* on rereading the classics, edited by Charles T. Lemert and Patricia T. Clough, Vol. 35, No.3, 1994, pp. 415–29
2 The phrase "guardian of identity" is originally that of the psychologist Erik Erikson. Ricoeur (1986, pp. 258–9) argues that interpretive theories of ideology imply theories of identity as I describe them here.
3 Althusser's translator, Ben Brewster, provides a glossary (pp. 249–58) in *For Marx* (1969) that includes "overdetermination" as it was used by Althusser. (Althusser also provides a brief response to the translator and to the glossary.) Brewster points to a borrowing from Freud for the concept. (Lacan's influence here and elsewhere in Althusser's work is also evident.) A representative text of Freud's in which the concept "overdetermination" appears is "Aetiology of Hysteria" (Freud [1896] 1989, p. 108): about the overdetermination of hysterical symptoms, Freud writes

"the idea which is selected for the production of a symptom is one which has been called up by a combination of several factors and which has been aroused from various directions simultaneously." George Ritzer (in his 1992 textbook *Sociological Theory*, New York, McGraw-Hill, p. 299) attributes Althusser's use of "overdetermination" to its use in Lenin and Mao. Yet it is more accurate to speak of the *logic* and not the concept itself in the writings of these authors, as is clear from Althusser's essay (1969, pp. 97ff.).

3 THE STRUCTURES OF KNOWLEDGES: THE FRENCH TRADITION

1 The term "cultural turn" is Roland Robertson's (1992, Ch. 2), whose treatment of the concept of culture in social science and social theory has influenced my own, particularly since it is informed by a sociology-of-knowledge perspective. Robertson's principal contribution is the implications of a theory of culture for the phenomenon of "globalization," a process he was one of the first to identify and to circumscribe as a problem, if not *the* problem of contemporary cultural sociology.

2 Lévi-Strauss (1976, pp. 622–63) refers to a "substantial identity" between language and culture: they are homologous because cultural phenomena have their source or origin in language. This is not the same thing as the claim that all signifying systems operate like languages, and are, indeed, languages. For a discussion of this "linguistic fallacy," see Krampen's (1979) and Gottdiener's (1985) discussions.

3 Michael Lane (1970, p. 436, n. 54) describes this unconscious operation of reason (*esprit*), pointing out that *esprit* is usually translated as "mind" by Jacobson and Schoepf. He translates it as "reason" to convey "the Cartesian nuance better."

4 See Edmund Leach's (1976) *Claude Lévi-Strauss*, pp. 23–7, for an exposition of the model; and Scheffler's (1966, pp. 66–8) discussion on the Prague school in modern structural linguistics. Lévi-Strauss himself has provided a graphic application of the model in an attempt to analyze cuisine. See "The Culinary Triangle" (1966b).

5 "Structure" can be defined as "a set of any elements between which, or between certain subsets of which, relations are defined" (Lane 1970, p. 24).

4 SELF KNOWLEDGES: THE AMERICAN TRADITION

1 For a systematic reflection on the importance of the Other for a social ontology of selfhood, see Perinbanayagam's "The Significance of the Other" (1985, Ch. 6).

2 In American sociology, the work of R. S. Perinbanayagam has consistently demonstrated the extent and depth of the influence of cultural forms in the fashioning of selfhood — from his study of self, society, and astrology in Jaffna, Sri Lanka (1982), to his *Signifying Acts* (1985), and *Discursive Acts* (1991).

3 Crapanzano (1992, pp. 75–7) claims that Mauss's lecture contains contradictory views on the universal or evolutionary (Crapanzano's terms) approach to the self.

5 ENGENDERED KNOWLEDGE: FEMINISM AND SCIENCE

1 Longino (1990, p. 129) distinguishes "androcentrism" (world perception from a man's standpoint that fails to accurately perceive or describe the lives of women) and "sexism" (practices that assume or legitimate the subordination of women to men). Harding's work, as with most other leading feminist writers, also employs this distinction (1986; 1991).

2 I am referring here to Longino's (1990, pp. 98–102) commentary on this and her identification of "constitution of an object" as Foucault's (1982). Among American pragmatist philosophers, especially George Herbert Mead, there is a theory remarkably similar to Foucault's, one that is equally "discursive" in emphasis. See Mead 1934, pp. 77–88; 1938, pp. 140–53; [1917] 1982.

3 See Rose (1994, pp. 88–9) and Harding (1991, pp. 82–3) for examples of this.

4 Behind these ideas and these political strategies lies the contemporary idea, in a "history of histories," that all writing of history is political. Hayden White (1973, "Introduction") has called this the "fictive character of historical reconstruction," a view that has challenged "history's claim among the sciences." The study and the writing of history has been given a "fictive" meaning in the sense that historical consciousness is viewed as an ideological stance or a "specifically Western prejudice" toward other "lesser" world cultures and civilizations.

5 This criticism regarding the claim of "epistemic privilege" has been particularly important, since it opened up standpoint theorists to the same criticisms leveled at men—namely, men's strategy of claiming the right to speak *for all* while rendering others silent in the process. I am indebted to Margaret Urban Walker for clarifying the implications of this issue, as well as for her careful reading of and commentary on this chapter.

6 For a particularly intense and unfriendly exchange between a leading standpoint theorist (Smith) and postmodernist feminist (Clough), see Smith (1993) and Clough (1993). Hilary Rose (1994, Ch. 4) has put together the two approaches in a most satisfactory manner, while remaining firmly in the camp of the standpoint theorists, asserting the importance and value of a "critical realism."

7 In the United States, "race" and "gender" have played important social and political roles, and of such a kind that popular culture and media play them up. "Ethnicity" probably takes second stage to "race" and "gender," in national politics at least, except in recent U.S. political and racial debates over immigrants and immigration, which tend to intensify in states such as California and Florida. But in the global arena, ethnic and national identities and struggles are currently paramount. When the leading U.S. sociologist and politician Daniel Patrick Moynihan published his most recent work on ethnicity, *Pandaemonium* (1993), its focus was global not national.

8 I am, of course, thinking of the important case of the Bangladeshi feminist writer Taslima Nasrin, who was forced into hiding when her government charged her with defaming Islam and when the mullahs put a price on her head. The case is not without its ironies, since Bangladesh's feminists also number among her enemies.

EPILOGUE: KNOWLEDGE AS CULTURE

1 Gunter Remmling opens his introductory essay, "Existence and Thought," to his edited collection *Towards the Sociology of Knowledge* (1973) with precisely this point. As Remmling indicates in his commentary, Arthur Child's (1940–1) essay

reveals how strongly and defensively academics working in both science and in the humanities reacted to the sociology of knowledge in its early years. Similarly, in two replies to Franz Adler, Werner Stark (1959) took the opportunity to emphatically defend his own methodological assumptions and positions.

2 The term "interpretive communities" is identified with Stanley Fish's (1980) *Is There a Text in this Class? The Authority of Interpretive Communities* (Cambridge, Massachusetts: Harvard University Press). It was used earlier by Janice Radway in 1974 in her study of romance literature, "Interpretive Communities and Variable Literacies: The Functions of Romance Reading" (*Daedalus* 113 (3); reprinted 1991 in C. Mukerji and M. Schudson (eds.) *Rethinking Popular Culture*, Berkeley: University of California Press).

3 Margaret Archer's "The Myth of Cultural Integration" (1988, Ch. 1) has demonstrated how the advance of "culture" as a key concept in sociology and sociological theory has been remarkable because of the term's extraordinary range and diversity of uses; "culture" has "displayed the weakest analytical development" of any other central concept in our discipline (p. 1).

4 Clyde Kluckhohn's introduction to anthropology, *Mirror for Man,* uses this holistic idea of culture, which was probably first used by Edward B. Tylor: "That complex whole which includes knowledge, belief, art, morals, law, custom" (Vol. 1 of Tylor's 1871 *Primitive Culture*). For discussions of these, see Geertz (1973, Ch. 1), Swidler (1986), and Archer (1988, Ch. 1).

REFERENCES

Alcoff, Linda, and Elizabeth Potter. 1993. *Feminist Epistemologies*. New York: Routledge.

Althusser, Louis. 1969. *For Marx*. Translated by B. Brewster. New York: Vintage/Random House.

————. 1971. *Lenin and Philosophy and Other Essays*. Translated by B. Brewster. New York: Monthly Review Press.

Anderson, Benedict. 1991. *Imagined Communities*. Revised edition. New York: Verso.

Angier, Natalie. 1994. "Feminists and Darwin: Scientists Try Closing the Gap." *The New York Times* (*Science Times*, 21 June): C1, C13.

Appiah, K. Anthony. 1994. "Identity, Authenticity, Survival: Multicultural Societies and Social Reproduction." Pp. 149–63 in C. Taylor *et al. Multiculturalism*. Princeton, New Jersey: Princeton University Press.

Archer, Margaret S. 1988. *Culture and Agency: The Place of Culture in Social Theory*. New York: Cambridge University Press.

Arendt, Hannah. 1968. *Totalitarianism*. Part 3 of *The Origins of Totalitarianism*. New York: Harcourt Brace & World.

Aronowitz, Stanley. 1988. *Science as Power: Discourse and Ideology in Modern Society*. Minneapolis: University of Minnesota Press.

————. 1990. *The Crisis in Historical Materialism*. Second edition. Minneapolis: University of Minnesota Press.

————. 1992. *The Politics of Identity: Class, Culture, and Social Movements*. New York: Routledge.

Bart, Pauline. 1971. "Sexism in Social Science." *Journal of Marriage and the Family* 33 (November): 734–45.

Barthes, Roland. [1953] 1968. *Writing Degree Zero*. Translated by A. Lavers and C. Smith. Preface by S. Sontag. New York: Hill & Wang.

————. [1957] 1972. *Mythologies*. Translated by A. Lavers. New York: Hill & Wang.

————. [1964] 1968. *Elements of Semiology*. Translated by A. Lavers and C. Smith. New York: Hill & Wang.

Beauvoir, Simone de. 1983. *The Second Sex*. Translated and edited by H. M. Parshley. New York: Alfred A. Knopf.

Belenky, Mary Field, Blythe McVicker Clinchy, Nancy Rule Goldberger, and Jill Mattuck Tarule. 1986. *Women's Ways of Knowing*. New York: Basic Books.

Bell, Daniel. 1976. *The Cultural Contradictions of Capitalism*. New York: Basic Books.

Benoist, Jean-Marie. 1978. *The Structural Revolution*. New York: St. Martin's Press.

Benton, James S. 1993. "Self and Society in Popular Social Criticism: 1920–1980." *Symbolic Interaction* 16 (2): 145–70.

Berger, Peter L. 1970. "Identity as a Problem in the Sociology of Knowledge." Pp. 373–84 in J. Curtis and J. Petras (eds.) *The Sociology of Knowledge*. New York: Praeger.
——. 1977. "Toward a Sociological Understanding of Psychoanalysis." Pp. 23–34 in P. L. Berger (ed.) *Facing Up To Modernity*. New York: Basic Books.
Berger, Peter L., and Thomas Luckmann. 1966. *The Social Construction of Reality*. New York: Doubleday.
Berger, Peter L., Brigitte Berger, and Hansfried Kellner. 1973. *The Homeless Mind: Modernization and Consciousness*. London and New York: Random House.
Berman, Marshall. 1982. *All That Is Solid Melts Into Air*. New York: Simon & Schuster.
——. 1992. "Why Modernism Still Matters." Pp. 33–58 in S. Lash and J. Friedman (eds.) *Modernity and Identity*. Boston: Blackwell.
Bernard, Jesse. 1973. "My Four Revolutions: An Autobiographical History of the American Sociological Association." *American Journal of Sociology* 78: 773–91.
Bernstein, Richard J. 1971. *Praxis and Action: Contemporary Philosophies of Human Activity*. Philadelphia: University of Pennsylvania Press.
——. 1983. *Beyond Objectivism and Relativism*. Philadelphia: University of Pennsylvania Press.
Best, Steven, and Douglas Kellner. 1991. *Postmodern Theory*. New York: The Guilford Press.
Bhabha, Homi K. 1994. *The Location of Culture*. New York: Routledge.
Billington, James H. 1980. *Fire in the Minds of Men*. New York: Basic Books.
Bleier, Ruth. 1984. *Science and Gender*. New York: Pergamon Press.
——. 1986. *Feminist Approaches to Science*. New York: Pergamon Press.
Bloor, David. 1991. *Knowledge and Social Imagery*. Second edition. Chicago, Illinois: University of Chicago Press.
Blumer, Herbert. 1969. *Symbolic Interactionism*. Englewood Cliffs, New Jersey: Prentice-Hall.
Boon, James. 1985. "Claude Lévi-Strauss." Pp. 161–76 in Q. Skinner (ed.) *The Return of Grand Theory in the Human Sciences*. New York: Columbia University Press.
Bordo, Susan. 1987. *The Flight to Objectivity*. Albany: State University of New York Press.
Boudon, Raymond. 1989. *The Analysis of Ideology*. New York: Oxford University Press.
Bowlby, John. 1969. *Attachment*. New York: Basic Books.
Braudy, Leo. 1986. *The Frenzy of Renown: Fame and its History*. New York. Oxford University Press.
Briggs, Asa. 1989. *Victorian Things*. Chicago, Illinois: University of Chicago Press.
Broverman, I. K., D. M. Broverman, F. E. Clarkson, P. S. Rosenkrantz, and S. R. Vogel. 1970. "Sex Role Stereotypes and Clinical Judgements of Mental Health." *Journal of Consulting and Clinical Psychology* 34: 1–7.
Brown, Richard Harvey. [1977] 1989. *A Poetic for Sociology*. Chicago, Illinois: University of Chicago Press.
——. 1987. *Society as Text*. Chicago, Illinois: University of Chicago Press.
——. 1992. *Writing the Social Text*. New York: Aldine De Gruyter.
Burckhardt, Jacob. [1890] 1954. *The Civilization of the Renaissance in Italy*. New York: The Modern Library.
Burke, Kenneth. 1989. *On Symbols and Society*. Edited and with an Introduction by Joseph R. Gusfield. Chicago, Illinois: University of Chicago Press.
Burke, Peter. 1992. "We, the People: Popular Culture and Popular Identity in Modern Europe." Pp. 293–308 in S. Lash and J. Friedman (eds.) *Modernity and Identity*. Cambridge, Massachusetts: Basil Blackwell.
Calhoun, Craig. 1991. "Indirect Relationships and Imagined Communities." Pp. 95–

117

121 in P. Bourdieu and J. Coleman (eds.) *Social Theory for a Changing Society*. Boulder, Colorado: Westview Press.

Carey, James W. 1988. *Communication as Culture*. Boston, Massachusetts: Unwin Hyman.

Child, Arthur. 1940–1. "The Theoretical Possibility of the Sociology of Knowledge." *Ethics* 51: 392–418.

Clarke, Robin. 1969. "Introduction." Pp. 9–17 in Daniel S. Greenberg *The Politics of American Science*. New York: Penguin.

Clifford, James. 1985. "On Ethnographic Self-Fashioning: Conrad and Malinowski" Pp. 140–62 in Thomas C. Heller, Morton Sosna, and David E. Wellbery (eds.) *Reconstructing Individualism*. Stanford, California: Stanford University Press.

——. 1986. "Introduction: Partial Truths." Pp. 1–26 in J. Clifford and G. E. Marcus *Writing Culture*. Berkeley: University of California Press.

——. 1988. *The Predicament of Culture*. Cambridge, Massachusetts: Harvard University Press.

Clifford, James, and George Marcus. 1986. *Writing Culture: The Poetics and Politics of Ethnography*. Berkeley: University of California Press.

Clough, Patricia T. 1992. *The End(s) of Ethnography*. Newbury Park, California: Sage.

——. 1993. "On the Brink of Deconstructing Sociology." *The Sociological Quarterly* 34 (1): 169–82.

Cohen, Joseph. 1989. "About Steaks Liking to Be Eaten." *Symbolic Interaction* 12 (2): 191–213.

——. 1993. "The Conflicting View of Symbolic Interactionists and Talcott Parsons Concerning the Nature of Relations between Persons and Nonhuman Objects." *Studies in Symbolic Interaction* 14: 127–53.

Collins, Patricia Hill. 1990. *Black Feminist Thought*. Boston, Massachusetts: Unwin Hyman.

Condorcet, Antoine-Nicolas, Marquis de [1794] 1973. *Sketch of the Progress of the Human Mind*. Excerpt, translated by J. Barraclough (1955). Pp. 800–10 in Peter Gay *The Enlightenment: A Comprehensive Anthology*. New York: Simon & Schuster.

Cooley, Charles H. [1909] 1983. *Social Organization*. New York: Schocken Books.

Crapanzano, Vincent. 1992. *Hermes' Dilemma and Hamlet's Desire*. Cambridge, Massachusetts: Harvard University Press.

Csikszentmihalyi, M., and E. Rochberg-Halton. 1981. *The Meaning of Things: Domestic Symbols and the Self*. Cambridge: Cambridge University Press.

Darnton, Robert. 1984. *The Great Cat Massacre*. New York: Vintage.

Davis, Fred. 1992. *Fashion, Culture, and Identity*. Chicago, Illinois: University of Chicago Press.

Denzin, Norman K. (1992) *Symbolic Interation and Cultural Studies: The Politics of Interpretation*. Cambridge, Massachusetts: Blackwell.

Derrida, Jacques. 1970. "Structure, Sign, and Play in the Discourse of the Human Sciences." Pp. 247–72 in R. Macksey and E. Donato (eds.) *The Language of Criticism and the Sciences of Man*. Baltimore, Maryland: The Johns Hopkins University Press.

——. 1992. "Widening Circles of Identification: Emotional Concerns in Sociogenetic Perspective." Unpublished paper.

Dewey, John. [1916] 1980. *Democracy and Education*. Vol. 9 of *Middle Works*. Carbondale: Southern Illinois University Press.

Dittmar, Helga. 1992. *The Social Psychology of Material Possessions: To Have Is to Be*. New York: St. Martin's Press.

Douglas, Mary. 1986. *How Institutions Think*. Syracuse, New York: Syracuse University Press.

Douglas, Mary, and Baron Isherwood. 1978. *The World of Goods*. New York: Basic Books.

Du Bois, W. E. B. [1903] 1989. *The Souls of Black Folk*. New York: Penguin.

Dumont, Louis. *Essays on Individualism*. Chicago, Illinois: University of Chicago Press.

Durkheim, Emile. [1893] 1933. *The Division of Labor in Society*. Translated by G. Simpson. New York: Free Press.

——. [1897] 1951. *Suicide*. Translated by J. A. Spaulding and G. Simpson. Edited and with an Introduction by G. Simpson. New York: Free Press.

——. [1897] 1982. "The Materialist Conception of History" (Review of Antonio Labriola). Pp. 167–74 in *The Rules of Sociological Method*." Edited by S. Lukes. Translated by W. D. Halls. New York: Free Press.

——. [1901] 1982. *The Rules of Sociological Method*. Edited by S. Lukes. Translated by W. D. Halls. New York: Free Press.

——. [1909] 1982. "The Contribution of Sociology to Psychology and Philosophy." Pp. 236–40 in *The Rules of Sociological Method*. Edited by S. Lukes. Translated by W. D. Halls. New York: Free Press.

——. [1914] 1983. *Pragmatism and Sociology*. Translated by J. C. Whitehouse. Edited by J. B. Allcock. New York: Columbia University Press.

——. 1915. *The Elementary Forms of the Religious Life*. Translated by J. W. Swain. London: George Allen & Unwin.

Durkheim, Emile and Marcel Mauss. 1963. *Primitive Classifications*. Translated and edited by R. Needham. Chicago, Illinois: University of Chicago Press.

Eagleton, Terry. 1991. *Ideology: An Introduction*. New York: Verso.

Elias, Norbert. 1978. *The Civilizing Process: The History of Manners*. New York: Urizen Books.

Engels, Friedrich. [1888] 1941. *Ludwig Feuerbach and the Outcome of German Classical Philosophy*. New York: International Publishers.

——. [1893] 1968. Letter to Franz Mehrling, 14 July 1893. Pp. 699–703 in Karl Marx and Friedrich Engels *Selected Works*. New York: International Publishers.

Farganis, Sondra. 1986. *Social Reconstruction of the Feminine Character*. Totowa, New Jersey: Rowman & Littlefield.

Featherstone, Mike. 1990. *Global Culture: Nationalism, Globalization and Modernity*. Newbury Park, California: Sage Publications.

Fee, Elizabeth. 1981. "Women's Nature and Scientific Objectivity." In M. Lowe and R. Hubbard (eds.) *Women's Nature: Rationalizations of Inequality*. New York: Pergamon Press.

——. 1986. "Critiques of Modern Science." Pp. 42–56 in R. Bleier (ed.) *Feminist Approaches to Science*. Oxford: Pergamon Press.

Foote, Nelson. [1951] 1970. "Identification as the Basis for a Theory of Motivation." Pp. 333–41 in G. P. Stone and H. Farberman (eds.) *Social Psychology through Symbolic Interaction*. New York: John Wiley.

Foucault, Michel. 1977. *Discipline and Punish*. Translated by A. Sheridan. New York: Pantheon.

——. 1980a. *An Introduction*. Vol. 1 of *The History of Sexuality*. New York: Random House/Vintage.

——. 1980b. *Power/Knowledge: Selected Interviews and Other Writings*. Edited by Colin Gordon. New York: Pantheon.

——. 1981. "Questions of Method: An Interview with Michel Foucault." *Ideology and Consciousness* 8 (Spring): 3–13.

——. 1982. *The Archeology of Knowledge*. Translated by A. M. Sheridan. New York: Pantheon.

——. 1984. "What is Enlightenment?" Pp. 32–50 in *The Foucault Reader*. Edited by Paul Rabinow. New York: Pantheon.

——. 1988. *Technologies of the Self*. Edited by L. H. Martin, H. Gutman, and P. H. Hutton. Amherst: University of Massachusetts Press.

Freud, Sigmund. [1896] 1989. "The Aetiology of Hysteria" (Abridged). Pp. 96–111 in Peter Gay (ed.) *The Freud Reader*. New York: W. W. Norton.

——. [1923] 1960. *The Ego and the Id*. New York: W. W. Norton.

Gadamer, Hans-Georg. 1975. *Truth and Method*. New York: Seabury.

Gay, Peter. 1969. *The Science of Freedom*. Vol. 2 of *The Enlightenment: An Interpretation*. New York: Alfred A. Knopf.

——. 1984. *Education of the Senses*. Vol. 1 of *The Bourgeois Experience: Victoria to Freud*. New York: Oxford University Press.

——. 1986. *The Tender Passion*. Vol. 2 of *The Bourgeois Experience: Victoria to Freud*. New York: Oxford University Press.

——. 1993. *The Cultivation of Hatred*. Vol. 3 of *The Bourgeois Experience: Victoria to Freud*. New York: Oxford University Press.

Geertz, Clifford. 1973. *The Interpretation of Cultures*. New York: Basic Books.

——. 1983. *Local Knowledge*. New York: Basic Books.

——. 1990. "A Lab of One's Own." *The New York Review of Books* (November 8): 19–23.

——. 1995. *After the Fact*. Cambridge, Massachusetts: Harvard University Press.

Gehlen, Arnold. [1949] 1980. *Man in the Age of Technology*. New York: Columbia University Press.

Gergen, Kenneth J. 1991. *The Saturated Self*. New York: Basic Books.

Gerth, Hans, and C. Wright Mills. 1946. "Introduction: The Man and his Work." Pp. 3–74 in *From Max Weber*. New York: Oxford.

Giddens, Anthony. 1984. *The Constitution of Society*. Berkeley: University of California Press.

——. 1990. *The Consequences of Modernity*. Stanford, California: Stanford University Press.

——. 1991. *Modernity and Self-Identity*. Stanford, California: Stanford University Press.

Gilligan, Carol. 1979. "Woman's Place in Man's Life-Cycle." *Harvard Educational Review* 49: 431–46.

——. 1982. *In a Different Voice*. Cambridge, Massachusetts: Harvard University Press.

Gottdiener, M. 1985. "Hegemony and Mass Culture: A Semiotic Approach." *American Journal of Sociology* 90 (5) (March): 979–1001.

Gouldner, Alvin W. 1970. *The Coming Crisis of Western Sociology*. New York: Basic Books.

——. 1976. *The Dialectic of Ideology and Technology*. New York: Seabury.

Greenblatt, Stephen. 1980. *Renaissance Self-Fashioning*. Chicago, Illinois: University of Chicago Press.

Hall, Stuart. 1980. "Cultural Studies and the Centre: Some Problematics and Problems." Pp. 15–47 in *Culture, Media, Language*. (*Working Papers in Cultural Studies*, 1972–9). London: Hutchinson, in association with the Centre for Contemporary Cultural Studies, University of Birmingham.

——. 1992. "Cultural Studies and its Theoretical Legacies." Pp. 277–86 in L. Grossberg, C. Nelson, and P. Treichler (eds.) *Cultural Studies*. New York: Routledge.

Haraway, Donna J. 1978. "Animal Sociology and a Natural Economy of the Body Politic" (Parts 1 and 2). *Signs* 4 (1): 21–36.

——. 1981. "In the Beginning Was the Word: The Genesis of Biological Theory." *Signs* 6 (3): 469–82.

——. 1988. "Situated Knowledges." *Feminist Studies* 14 (3): 575–99.

——. 1989. *Primate Visions: Gender, Race, and Nature in the World of Modern Science*. New York: Routledge.

——. 1991. *Simians, Cyborgs, and Women*. New York: Routledge.

Harding, Sandra. 1986. *The Science Question in Feminism*. Ithaca, New York: Cornell University Press.

——. 1990. "Feminism, Science, and the Anti-Enlightenment Critiques." Pp. 83–106 in Linda J. Nicholson (ed.) *Feminism/Postmodernism*. Introduction by L. J. Nicholson. New York: Routledge.

——. 1991. *Whose Science? Whose Knowledge?* Ithaca, New York: Cornell University Press.

——. 1993a. "Rethinking Standpoint Epistemology." Pp. 49–82 in L. Alcoff and E. Potter (eds.) *Feminist Epistemologies*. New York: Routledge.

——. 1993b. "Reinventing Ourselves as Other." Pp. 140–64 in L. S. Kaufman (ed.) *American Feminist Thought at Century's End*. Boston, Massachusetts: Blackwell.

Harding, Sandra, and Merrill Hintikka. 1983. *Discovering Reality: Feminist Perspectives on Epistemology, Metaphysics, Methodology and Philosophy of Science*. Dordrecht: Reidel.

Harland, Richard. 1987. *Superstructuralism: The Philosophy of Structuralism and Post-Structuralism*. London: Methuen.

Hartsock, Nancy. 1983. "The Feminist Standpoint: Developing the Ground for a Specifically Feminist Historical Materialism." Pp. 283–310 in S. Harding and M. Hintikka *Discovering Reality*. Dordrecht: Reidel.

Heller, Thomas C., Morton Sosna, and David E. Wellerby. 1986. *Reconstructing Individualism*. Stanford, California: Stanford University Press.

Hilts, Philip J. 1991. "Hero in Exposing Science Hoax Paid Dearly." *The New York Times* (22 March): 1, B6.

——. 1992. "The Science Mob." *The New Republic* (18 May): 24–31.

Hochschild, Arlie Russell. 1983. *The Managed Heart*. Berkeley: University of California Press.

Hrdy, Sarah. 1981. *The Women That Never Evolved*. Cambridge, Massachusetts: Harvard University Press.

Hubbard, Ruth. 1990. *The Politics of Women's Biology*. New Brunswick, New Jersey: Rutgers University Press.

Hubbard, Ruth, M. S. Henifin, and Barbara Fried. 1982. *Biological Woman: The Convenient Myth*. Cambridge, Massachusetts: Schenkman. (Earlier version published 1979 under the title *Women Look at Biology Looking at Women*.)

Hughes, Robert. 1993. *The Culture of Complaint*. New York: Oxford University Press.

Hunt, Lynn. 1989. *The New Cultural History*. Edited with an Introduction by Lynn Hunt. Berkeley: University of California Press.

Hutcheon, Linda. 1988. *A Poetics of Postmodernism*. New York: Routledge.

Janssen-Jurreit, M. 1980. *Sexism: The Male Monopoly on History and Thought*. New York: Farrar, Straus & Giroux.

Joas, Hans. 1985. *G. H. Mead: A Contemporary Re-Examination of his Thought*. Translated by R. Meyer. Cambridge, Massachusetts: The MIT Press.

Keller, Evelyn Fox. 1978. "Gender and Science." *Psychoanalysis and Contemporary Thought* 1: 409–33.

——. 1985. *Reflections on Gender and Science*. New Haven, Connecticut: Yale University Press.

Kleinman, Arthur. 1988. *Rethinking Psychiatry: From Cultural Category to Personal Experience*. New York: Free Press.

Knorr-Cetina, Karin. 1993. "Laboratory Studies: The Cultural Approach to the Study of Science." Paper presented at the annual meeting of the American Sociological Association (Miami, Florida).

Kozol, Jonathan. 1991. *Savage Inequalities: Children in America's Schools*. New York: HarperCollins.

Krampen, Martin. 1979. *Meaning in the Urban Environment*. London: Pion.

Kuhn, Thomas S. 1970. *The Structure of Scientific Revolutions*. Second edition. Chicago, Illinois: University of Chicago Press.

Kurzweil, Edith. 1980. *The Age of Structuralism: From Lévi-Strauss to Foucault*. New York: Columbia University Press.

Lane, Michael. 1970. *Introduction to Structuralism*. New York: Basic Books.

Leach, Edmund. 1976. *Claude Lévi-Strauss*. Revised edition. Harmondsworth: Penguin.

Lemert, Charles. 1990. "The Uses of French Structuralism in Sociology." Pp. 230–54 in G. Ritzer (ed.) *Frontiers of Social Theory*. New York: Columbia University Press.

——. 1991. "The End of Ideology, Really." *Sociological Theory* 9 (2): 164–72.

——. 1994. "Social Theory at the End of a Short Century." *Sociological Theory* 12 (2): 140–52.

Lemert, Charles, and Patricia T. Clough. 1994. "Lost Classics and Their Future in Sociology." *Sociological Quarterly* (Special Issue) 35 (3): i–iv.

Lerner, Gerda. 1986. *The Creation of Patriarchy*. New York: Oxford University Press.

Lévi-Strauss, Claude. 1945. "French Sociology." Pp. 503–37 in Georges Gurvitch and Wilbert E. Moore (eds.) *Twentieth Century Sociology*. New York: The Philosophical Library.

——. [1950] 1968. "Introduction à l'oeuvre de Marcel Mauss." Pp. xi–lii in M. Mauss *Sociologie et Anthropologie*. Paris: Universitaires de France.

——. [1955] 1977. *Tristes Tropiques*. Translated by J. and D. Weightman. New York: Pocket Books.

——. [1962] 1969. *Totemism*. Translated by R. Needham. Introduction by R. C. Poole. New York: Penguin.

——. 1963. *Structural Anthropology*. Vol. 1. Translated by C. Jacobson and B. G. Schoepf. New York: Basic Books.

——. [1964] 1969. *The Raw and the Cooked: Introduction to a Science of Mythology*. Vol. 1. Translated by J. and D. Weightman. New York: Harper & Row.

——. 1966a. *The Savage Mind*. Chicago, Illinois: University of Chicago Press.

——. 1966b. "The Culinary Triangle." *New Society* [London] (22 December): 937–40.

——. 1968. *The Scope of Anthropology*. Translated by S. O. Paul and R. A. Paul. London: Jonathan Cape.

——. 1976. *Structural Anthropology*. Vol. 2. Translated by M. Layton. Chicago, Illinois: University of Chicago Press.

——. 1982. *The Way of Masks*. Translated by S. Modelski. Seattle, Washington: University of Washington Press.

Lukes, Steven. 1972. *Emile Durkheim: His Life and Work*. New York: Harper & Row.

Lofland, John. 1993. *Polite Protesters*. Ithaca, New York: Cornell University Press.

Longino, Helen E. 1990. *Science as Social Knowledge*. Princeton, New Jersey: Princeton University Press.

Longino, Helen E., and Ruth Doell. 1983. "Body, Bias and Behavior: A Comparative Analysis of Reasoning in Two Areas of Biological Science." *Signs* 9 (2): 206–27.

Lukács, Georg. [1911] 1968. *History and Class Consciousness*. Translated by Rodney Livingstone. Cambridge, Massachusetts: The MIT Press.

Lyotard, Jean-François. 1984. *The Postmodern Condition: A Report on Knowledge*.

REFERENCES

Translated by G. Bennington and B. Massumi. Foreword by F. Jameson. Minneapolis: University of Minnesota Press.

Mannheim, Karl. [1924] 1952. "Historicism." Pp. 84–133 in P. Kecskemeti (ed.) *Essays on the Sociology of Knowledge*. London: Routledge & Kegan Paul.

———. 1936. *Ideology and Utopia*. New York: Harcourt Brace & World.

Marcus, George E., and Michael M. Fisher. 1986. *Anthropology as Cultural Critique*. Chicago, Illinois: University of Chicago Press.

Marx, Karl. [1846–7] 1936. *The Poverty of Philosophy*. Edited by C. P. Dutt and V. Chattopadhyaya. New York: International Publishers.

———. [1859] 1975. "Preface to *A Contribution to the Critique of Political Economy*." Pp. 424–8 in *Karl Marx: Early Writings*. New York: Vintage Books.

———. [1869] 1963. *The 18th Brumaire of Louis Bonaparte*. New York: International Publishers.

Marx, Karl, and Friedrich Engels. [1845–6] 1970. *The German Ideology*. Part 1. Edited and with an Introduction by C. J. Arthur. New York: International Publishers.

———. [1888] 1967. *The Communist Manifesto*. New York: Seabury.

———. 1968. *Selected Works*. New York: International Publishers.

Mauss, Marcel. [1938] 1979. *Sociology and Psychology*. Translated by B. Brewster. Boston, Massachusetts: Routledge & Kegan Paul.

Mead, George Herbert. 1903. "The Definition of the Psychical." *Decennial Publications of the University of Chicago*. First Series, Vol. 3: 77–112.

———. [1908] 1964. "The Philosophical Basis of Ethics." Pp. 82–93 in *Selected Writings of G. H. Mead*. Edited by A. Reck. New York: Bobbs–Merrill.

———. [1909] 1964. "Social Psychology as Counterpart to Physiological Psychology." Pp. 94–104 in *Selected Writings of G. H. Mead*. Edited by A. Reck. New York: Bobbs–Merrill.

———. [1910] 1964. "What Social Objects Must Psychology Presuppose?" Pp. 105–13 in *Selected Writings of G. H. Mead*. Edited by A. Reck. New York: Bobbs–Merrill.

———. [1913] 1964. "The Social Self." Pp.142–9 in *Selected Writings of G. H. Mead*. Edited by A. Reck. New York: Bobbs–Merrill.

———. [1914] 1982. "The 1914 Class Lectures in Social Psychology." Pp. 27–105 in *The Individual and the Social Self: Unpublished Work of G. H. Mead*. Edited by David L. Miller. Chicago, Illinois: University of Chicago Press.

———. [1917] 1982. "Consciousness of Mind, the Self, and Scientific Objects." Pp. 176–96 in *The Individual and the Social Self: Unpublished Work of G. H. Mead*. Edited by David L. Miller. Chicago, Illinois: University of Chicago Press.

———. [1922] 1964. "A Behavioristic Account of the Significant Symbol." Pp. 240–7 in *Selected Writings of G. H. Mead*. Edited by A. Reck. New York: Bobbs–Merrill.

———. [1924–5] 1964. "The Genesis of Self and Social Control." Pp. 267–93 in *Selected Writings of G. H. Mead*. Edited by A. Reck. New York: Bobbs–Merrill.

———. 1932. *The Philosophy of the Present*. Chicago, Illinois: University of Chicago Press.

———. 1934. *Mind, Self, and Society*. Chicago, Illinois: University of Chicago Press.

———. 1936. *Movements of Thought in the Nineteenth Century*. Edited by M. H. Moore. Chicago, Illinois: University of Chicago Press.

———. 1938. *The Philosophy of the Act*. Chicago, Illinois: University of Chicago Press.

Merchant, Carolyn. 1980. *The Death of Nature*. San Francisco, California: Harper & Row.

Merton, Robert K. 1949. "The Sociology of Knowledge." Pp. 217–45 in R.K. Merton *Social Theory and Social Structure*. Glencoe, Illinois: The Free Press.

———. [1942] 1990. "The Normative Structure of Science." Pp. 67–74 in J. C.

Alexander and S. Seidman (eds.) *Culture and Society*. New York: Cambridge University Press.

Miller, David. 1973. *George Herbert Mead: Self, Language, and the World*. Chicago, Illinois: University of Chicago Press.

Mills, C. Wright. 1939. "Language, Logic, and Culture." *American Sociological Review* 4 (October): 670–80.

———. 1940. "Methodological Consequences of the Sociology of Knowledge." *American Journal of Sociology* 46 (3) (November): 316–30.

———. 1959. *The Sociological Imagination*. New York: Oxford University Press.

Moore, Barrington, Jr. 1978. *Injustice: The Social Bases of Obedience and Revolt*. White Plains, New York: M. E. Sharpe.

Moynihan, Daniel Patrick. 1993. *Pandaemonium: Ethnicity in International Politics*. New York: Oxford University Press.

National Science Foundation. 1982. *Women and Minorities in Science and Engineering*. Washington, D.C.: National Science Foundation.

Nicholson, Linda J. 1990. *Feminism/Postmodernism*. New York: Routledge.

Nisbet, Robert. 1980. *History of the Idea of Progress*. New York: Basic Books.

Oakes, Guy. 1988. "Farewell to *The Protestant Ethic?*" (Symposium on Max Weber). *Telos* 78: 81–94.

Park, Robert E. 1950. *Race and Culture*. Vol. 1 of *The Collected Papers of Robert Ezra Park*. Edited by E. C. Hughes, C. S. Johnson, J. Masuoka, R. Redfield, and L. Wirth. Glencoe, Illinois: Free Press.

———. 1967. *On Social Control and Collective Behavior*. Edited and with an Introduction by Ralph H. Turner. Chicago, Illinois: University of Chicago Press.

Parker, A., M. Russo, D. Sommer, and P. Yaeger. 1992. *Nationalities and Sexualities*. New York: Routledge.

Percy, Walker. 1958. "Symbol, Consciousness and Intersubjectivity." *Journal of Philosophy* 5: 631–41.

Perinbanayagam, R. S. 1982. *The Karmic Theater*. Amherst: University of Massachusetts Press.

———. 1985. *Signifying Acts*. Carbondale: Southern Illinois University Press.

———. 1991. *Discursive Acts*. New York: Aldine De Gruyter.

Peterson, Richard A. 1976. "The Production of Culture: A Prolegomenon." Pp. 7–22 in R. A. Peterson (ed.) *The Production of Culture*. Beverly Hills, California: Sage Publications.

———. 1994. "Cultural Studies through the Production Perspective: Progress and Prospects." Pp. 191–220 in D. Crane (ed.) *The Sociology of Culture*. Cambridge, Massachusetts: Blackwell.

Poole, Roger C. 1969. "Introduction" to C. Lévi-Strauss *Totemism*. New York: Penguin.

Remmling, Gunter. 1973. *Towards the Sociology of Knowledge*. London: Routledge & Kegan Paul.

Rich, Adrienne. 1977. "Conditions for Work: The Common World of Women." Pp. xiv–xxiv in S. Ruddick and P. Daniels (eds.) *Working it Out*. New York: Pantheon.

Ricoeur, Paul. 1976. *Interpretation Theory: Discourse and the Surplus of Meaning*. Fort Worth: Texas Christian University Press.

———. 1986. *Lectures on Ideology and Utopia*. Edited by George H. Taylor. New York: Columbia University Press.

Riesman, David. 1954. *Individualism Reconsidered*. Glencoe, Illinois: Free Press.

Riesman, David, with Nathan Glazer and Reuel Denney. 1950. *The Lonely Crowd*. New Haven, Connecticut: Yale University Press.

Robertson, Roland. 1992. *Globalization: Social Theory and Global Culture*. Newbury Park, California: Sage Publications.

———. 1993. "Cultural Relativity and Social Theory." Pp. 84–96 in E. Leonard, H. Strasser, and K. Westhues (eds.) *In Search of Community: Essays in Memory of Werner Stark, 1909–1985*. New York: Fordham University Press.

Rock, Paul. 1979. *The Making of Symbolic Interaction*. Totowa, New Jersey: Rowman & Littlefield.

Rorty, Richard. 1979. *Philosophy and the Mirror of Nature*. Princeton, New Jersey: Princeton University Press.

———. 1982. *Consequences of Pragmatism: Essays, 1972–1980*. Minneapolis: University of Minnesota Press.

Rosaldo, Michelle Zimbalist, and Louise Lamphere. 1974. *Woman, Culture, and Society*. Stanford, California: Stanford University Press.

Rose, Hilary. 1983. "Hand, Brain and Heart: Towards a Feminist Epistemology for the Natural Sciences." *Signs* 9 (1): 73–96.

———. 1986. "Beyond Masculinist Realities." Pp. 57–76 in R. Bleier (ed.) *Feminist Approaches to Science*. Oxford: Pergamon Press.

———. 1994. *Love, Power and Knowledge*. Bloomington: Indiana University Press.

Rose, Hilary, and Steven Rose. 1969. *Science and Society*. London and Harmondsworth: Allen Lane and Penguin.

———. 1979. *Ideology of/in the Natural Sciences*. Cambridge, Massachusetts: Schenkman.

Rosser, Sue V. 1986. "The Relationship between Women's Studies and Science." Pp. 165–80 in R. Bleier (ed.) *Feminist Approaches to Science*. New York: Pergamon Press.

Rossi, Alice. 1965. "Women in Science: Why So Few?" *Science* 148 (3674): 1196–202.

Rossiter, Margaret. 1982. *Women Scientists in America: Struggles and Strategies to 1940*. Baltimore, Maryland: The Johns Hopkins University Press.

Sahlins, Marshall. 1976. *Culture and Practical Reason*. Chicago, Illinois: University of Chicago Press.

———. 1985. *Islands of History*. Chicago, Illinois: University of Chicago Press.

Said, Edward W. 1983. *The World, the Text, and the Critic*. Cambridge, Massachusetts: Harvard University Press.

Saussure, Ferdinand de. 1966. *Course in General Linguistics*. Edited by C. Bally and A. Sechehaye, in collaboration with A. Riedlinger. Translated by W. Baskin. New York: McGraw–Hill.

Schachtel, Ernest G. 1959. *Metamorphosis*. New York: Basic Books.

Scheffler, Harold W. 1966. "Structuralism in Anthropology." Pp. 56–78 in *Structuralism*. Edited and with an Introduction by Jacques Ehrmann. New York: Doubleday.

Scheler, Max. [1924] 1980. *Problems of a Sociology of Knowledge*. Translated by M. S. Frings. Edited and with an Introduction by K. W. Stikkers. London: Routledge & Kegan Paul.

———. 1992. *On Feeling, Knowing, and Valuing*. Edited and with an Introduction by H. J. Bershady. Chicago, Illinois: University of Chicago Press.

Schickel, Richard. 1986. *Intimate Strangers: The Culture of Celebrity*. New York: Fromm International Publishing Co.

Schneewind, J. B. 1986. "The Use of Autonomy in Ethical Theory." Pp. 64–75 in T. C. Heller, M. Sosna, and D. E. Wellbery (eds.) *Reconstructing Individualism*. Stanford, California: Stanford University Press.

Schutz, Alfred. 1971. *The Problem of Social Reality*. Vol. 1 of *Collected Papers*. Edited by M. Natanson. The Hague: Martinus Nijhoff.

Seidman, Steven. 1991. "The End of Sociological Theory: The Postmodern Hope." *Sociological Theory* 9 (2): 131–46.

Shalin, Dmitri. 1986. "Pragmatism and Social Interactionism." *American Sociological Review* 51: 9–29.

Sherif, Carolyn Wood. 1979. "Bias in Psychology." Pp. 93-133 in J. A. Sherman and E. T. Beck (eds.) *The Prism of Sex*. Madison: University of Wisconsin Press.

Shils, Edward. 1981. *Tradition*. Chicago, Illinois: University of Chicago Press.

Sichtermann, Barbara. 1986. *Femininity: The Politics of the Personal*. Cambridge: Polity Press.

Signs: Journal of Women in Culture and Society. 1978. Special issue on women and science, 4 (1).

Simmel, Georg. [1908] 1950. "Adornment." Pp. 338–44 in *The Sociology of Georg Simmel*. Edited by K. Wolff. New York: Free Press.

Smith, Dorothy E. 1987. *The Everyday World as Problematic*. Boston, Massachusetts: Northeastern University Press.

——. 1990a. *The Conceptual Practices of Power: A Feminist Sociology of Knowledge*. Boston, Massachusetts: Northeastern University Press.

——. 1990b. *Texts, Facts, and Femininity: Exploring the Relations of Ruling*. New York: Routledge.

——. 1993. "High Noon in Textland: A Critique of Clough." *The Sociological Quarterly* 34 (1): 183–92.

Sombart, Werner. 1928. *Der Moderne Kapitallismus*. Seventh edition in 6 Vols. Condensed translation and Introduction (1933) by F. L. Nussbaum as *A History of the Economic Institutions of Modern Europe*. New York: F. S. Crofts & Co.

Sontag, Susan. 1968. "Preface" to R. Barthes *Writing Degree Zero*. Translated by A. Lavers and C. Smith. New York: Hill & Wang.

Stark, Werner. [1958] 1991. *The Sociology of Knowledge*. With a New Introduction by E. Doyle McCarthy. New Brunswick, New Jersey: Transaction Books.

——. 1959. "Reply." *Kyklos* 12 (2–3): 221–6, 506–9.

——. 1980. *Safeguards of the Social Bond, Custom and Law*. Vol. 3 of *The Social Bond*. New York: Fordham University Press.

Stehr, Nico, and Volker Meja. 1984. *Society and Knowledge*. New Brunswick, New Jersey: Transaction Books.

Steiner, George. 1967. *Language and Silence*. New York: Atheneum.

Stikkers, Kenneth. 1980. "Introduction." Pp. 1–30 in Max Scheler *Problems of a Sociology of Knowledge*. London: Routledge & Kegan Paul.

Stone, Lawrence. 1994. "The Use and Abuse of Herstory." *The New Republic* (2 May): 31–7.

Summer, William Graham. [1906] 1940. *Folkways*. New York: New American Library.

Swaan, Abram de. 1990. *The Management of Normality*. New York: Routledge.

Swidler, Ann. 1986. "Culture in Action: Symbols and Strategies." *American Sociological Review* 51 (April): 273–86.

Swidler, Ann, and Jorge Arditi. 1994. "The New Sociology of Knowledge." *Annual Review of Sociology* 20: 305–29.

Taylor, Charles. 1989. *Sources of the Self: The Making of the Modern Identity*. Cambridge, Massachusetts: Harvard University Press.

Taylor, Charles, K. Anthony Appiah, Jürgen Habermas, Steven C. Rockefeller, Michael Walzer, and Susan Wolf. 1994. *Multiculturalism*. Edited and with an Introduction by Amy Guttmann. Princeton, New Jersey: Princeton University Press.

Therborn, Goran. 1980 *The Ideology of Power and the Power of Ideology*. London: New Left Books.

Thompson, E. P. 1963. *The Making of the English Working Class*. London: Gollancz.

REFERENCES

Thompson, John B. 1990. *Ideology and Modern Culture*. Stanford, California: Stanford University Press.

Thompson, Kenneth. 1986. *Beliefs and Ideology*. London: Tavistock.

Tocqueville, Alexis de. [1835, 1840] 1990. *Democracy in America*. Vols I and II. New York: Vintage Books.

Veblen, Thorstein. [1899] 1967. *The Theory of the Leisure Class*. With an Introduction by R. Lekachman. New York: Viking.

Vetter, B. 1980. "Sex Discrimination in the Halls of Science." *Chemical and Engineering News* (March): 37–8.

Wagner, Roy. 1981. *The Invention of Culture*. Revised and expanded edition. Chicago, Illinois: University of Chicago Press.

Walker, Margaret Urban. 1991. "Partial Consideration." *Ethics* 101 (4): 758–74.

——. 1992. "Feminism, Ethics, and the Question of Theory." *Hypatia* 7 (3): 23–38.

Wallerstein, Immanuel. 1990. "Culture as the Ideological Battleground of the Modern World-System." Pp. 31–56 in Mike Featherstone (ed.) *Global Culture*. Newbury Park, California: Sage Publications.

Webber, M. W. 1967. "Order in Diversity: Community without Propinquity." Pp. 29–54 in L. Wirigo (ed.) *Cities and Space*. Baltimore, Maryland: The Johns Hopkins University Press.

Weber, Max. [1904–5] 1958. *The Protestant Ethic and the Spirit of Capitalism*. Translated by T. Parsons. Foreword by R. H. Tawney. New York: Charles Scribner's Sons.

Weigert, Andrew. 1986. *Society and Identity*. New York: Cambridge University Press.

Weisstein, Naomi. 1977. "Adventures of a Woman in Science." Pp. 242–50 in S. Ruddick and P. Daniels (eds.) *Working it Out*. New York: Pantheon.

White, Hayden. 1973. *Metahistory: The Historical Imagination in Nineteenth-Century Europe*. Baltimore, Maryland: The Johns Hopkins University Press.

Williams, Raymond. 1981. *The Sociology of Culture*. New York: Schocken Books.

——. 1983. *Keywords*. New York: Oxford University Press.

Woolf, Virginia. [1938] 1966. *Three Guineas*. New York: Harcourt Brace Jovanovich.

Znaniecki, Florian. [1940] 1970. "Sociology and Theory of Knowledge." Pp. 307–19 in J. E. Curtis and J. W. Petras (eds.) *The Sociology of Knowledge*. New York: Praeger.

INDEX